Using Playful Practice to Comm Special Children

Playfulness   portant; it creates an alternative space where emotional, cognitive and social
dimensions   be explored and tested. This highly practical book explores the endless possibilities of us   playful, creative and interactive activities to meaningfully engage with children
with severe   found or multiple learning difficulties or autism spectrum disorders.

The auth   presents playfulness as 'an experimental frame of mind', and encourages practitioners to   y with roles, ideas, words, concepts and objects in order to enhance relationships
and interve   ons. By providing accessible steps to playfulness, this text explores some of the
contempora   issues surrounding the education of children with severe learning-needs, in
particular th   use of 'intensive interaction'.

This tex   onsiders different areas of creative interactive work for practitioners to draw
inspiration   m, including:

- musi
- intera   ve musical movement
- finge   nce
- story   d drama
- artwo
- reflec   circle.

The varied   ay of tried-and-tested original activities have been devised to encourage the
developmen   f social interaction, cognition, play, experimentation and creativity, in particular, but not   lusively, for children whose learning needs are more complex. The author also
invites teac   s working in mainstream education, particularly early years and primary, to
investigate   creative possibilities inherent in playfulness and to use the activities in this book
to enhance   e learning environment.

This tex   ffers an abundance of advice, practical strategies and tips for teachers working in
special and   instream early years and primary education. Practitioners such as therapists, care
workers, co   munity musicians and creative arts specialists will also find this book useful.

Margaret Corke is a play and creative arts therapist, interactive music specialist, teaching
assistant, consultant and freelance trainer. She has previously authored *Approaches to
Communication through Music* (2002), also published by Routledge.

nasen
Helping Everyone Achieve

Other titles published in association with the National Association for Special Educational Needs (nasen):

Forthcoming titles:

Language for Learning in the Secondary School: A Practical Guide for Supporting Students with Speech, Language and Communication Needs
Sue Hayden and Emma Jordan
2012/pb: 978-0-415-61975-2

ADHD: All Your Questions Answered: A Complete Handbook for SENCOs and Teachers
Fintan O'Regan
2012/pb: 978-0-415-59770-8

Assessing Children with Specific Learning Difficulties: A Teacher's Practical Guide
Gavin Reid, Gad Elbeheri and John Everatt
2012/pb: 978-0-415-67027-2

Creating Multisensory Environments: Practical Ideas for Teaching and Learning
Christopher Davies
2012/pb: 978-0-415-57330-6

The Equality Act for Educational Professionals: A Simple Guide to Disability and Inclusion in Schools
Geraldine Hills
2012/pb: 978-0-415-68768-3

More Trouble with Maths: A Teacher's Complete Guide to Identifying and Diagnosing Mathematical Difficulties
Steve Chinn
2012/pb: 978-0-415-67013-5

Dyslexia and Inclusion: Classroom Approaches for Assessment, Teaching and Learning
Gavin Reid
2012/pb: 978-0-415-60758-2

Available now:

Brilliant Ideas for Using ICT in the Inclusive Classroom
Sally McKeown and Angela McGlashon
2011/pb: 978-0-415-67254-2

The SENCO Survival Guide: The Nuts and Bolts of Everything You Need to Know
Sylvia Edwards
2010/pb: 978-0-415-59281-9

The SEN Handbook for Trainee Teachers, NQTs and Teaching Assistants
Wendy Spooner
2010/pb: 978-0-415-56771-8

Attention Deficit Hyperactivity Disorder: What Can Teachers Do?
Geoff Kewley
2010/pb: 978-0-415-49202-7

Young People with Anti-social Behaviours: Practical Resources for Professionals
Kathy Hampson
2010/pb: 978-0-415-56570-7

Confronting Obstacles to Inclusion: International Responses to Developing Inclusive Education
Richard Rose
2010/pb: 978-0-415-49363-5

Supporting Children's Reading: A Complete Short Course for Teaching Assistants, Volunteer Helpers and Parents
Margaret Hughes and Peter Guppy
2010/pb: 978-0-415-49836-4

Dyspraxia 5–14: Identifying and Supporting Young People with Movement Difficulties
Christine Macintyre
2009/pb: 978-0-415-54396-5

A Handbook for Inclusion Managers: Steering Your School towards Inclusion
Ann Sydney
2009/pb: 978-0-415-49198-3

Living with Dyslexia: The Social and Emotional Consequences of Specific Learning Difficulties/Disabilities
Barbara Riddick and Angela Fawcett
2009/pb: 978-0-415-47758-1

Using Playful Practice to Communicate with Special Children

Margaret Corke

LONDON AND NEW YORK

Helping Everyone Achieve

First published 2012
by Routledge
2 Park Square, Milton Park, Abingdon, Oxon OX14 4RN

Simultaneously published in the USA and Canada
by Routledge
711 Third Avenue, New York, NY 10017

Routledge is an imprint of the Taylor & Francis Group, an informa business

British Library Cataloguing in Publication Data
A catalogue record for this book is available from the British Library

Library of Congress Cataloging in Publication Data
Corke, Margaret.
Using playful practice to communicate with special children / Margaret Corke.
p. cm. — (David Fulton / nasen)
Includes bibliographical references and index.
1. Learning disabled children—Education. 2. Learning disabled children—Recreation.
3. Early childhood special education. 4. Communication in education. 5. Creative activities
and seat work. I. Title.
LC4704.C685 2012
371.9—dc23
2011023345

ISBN: 978-0-415-68766-9 (hbk)
ISBN: 978-0-415-68767-6 (pbk)
ISBN: 978-0-203-15422-9 (ebk)

Typeset in Bembo
by FiSH Books, Enfield

MIX
Paper from
responsible sources
FSC
www.fsc.org   FSC® C004839

Printed and bound in Great Britain by
TJ International Ltd, Padstow, Cornwall

nasen is a professional membership association that supports all those who work with or care for children and young people with special and additional educational needs. Members include teachers, teaching assistants, support workers, other educationalists, students and parents.

nasen supports its members through policy documents, journals, its magazine *Special!*, publications, professional development courses, regional networks and newsletters. Its website contains more current information such as responses to government consultations. **nasen**'s published documents are held in very high regard both in the UK and internationally.

Contents

Foreword

Teachers and support staff arrive at school every day with a commitment to the learning experiences and development of children and young people with extra-special educational needs. There is a huge and sometimes indescribable reward for working with this group of children but it is important to also acknowledge that this work is hard. Progress is often discrete and the challenges at times unpredictable. Practitioners find themselves continually searching for new ideas and activities to keep their classrooms and work streams alive. Those of us who are lucky will have worked alongside practitioners with an extraordinary passion for learning, both in themselves and the children they teach. Margaret is one of these people and she continues to inspire, share and lead us within this special field.

In my experience, the most successful sessions are those where I can be playful with the children I work with. Playfulness and a child's ability to be playful indicate to me the potential for learning. Working directly with children as well as practitioners has shown me that the potential for learning not only rests on the child but also on the practitioners who work with them on a day-to-day basis.

As many of us know, children experience playfulness in different ways. Many of the children we work with do not develop in a predictable way. This book reminds us that every learner has a spark that can be nurtured into a playful routine. Margaret inspires us to search for those responses and behaviours that invite us to be playful with the learners we work with.

This book teaches us that key to playfulness is taking the child's lead. What is fun for them – a spin, a tickle, a room full of bubbles? Is there a better feeling than when a learner allows you into their game? This is especially true of those learners with autism spectrum disorders who at times may appear to tolerate so little from the outside world. Is this because our idea of the world, and particularly of what is fun and of interest, is so different from their own? Being prepared to engage in playful behaviour may provide a rare opportunity to share a special understanding of their world.

To the inexperienced eye, playfulness may, at best, look like fun and, at worst, a poor use of time. Having had the opportunity to work and learn alongside Margaret I am reassured that playfulness is, from a developmental point of view, the most appropriate and useful skill we may master when working with learners with complex learning and communication needs.

In my view this book is not necessarily going to teach you how to be playful, though Margaret's activity ideas will definitely give you a boost. For me, this book reminds me, quite simply, that playfulness is inside all of us; but, more importantly, it reminds me that we have permission to play. This book has made me smile and nod, and aside from being a truly enjoyable read it provides me with the evidence base for something that I have been doing for years.

Hannah Lewis
(highly specialist speech and language therapist)

Acknowledgements

Gratitude goes to Eric, my incredibly lovely supportive husband, who quietly wills me on, every step of the way

I owe a special debt of gratitude to Hannah Lewis (specialist speech and language therapist), who has gently 'walked' beside me during the process of writing this book. She has always been thoughtful and candid in her comments and this has helped to guide the process. Many of Hannah's insights are, inevitably, woven into the fabric of this text – she has taught me a great deal. The time and effort she has given to this project mirror her unwavering commitment to the care, education and well-being of people with significant intellectual impairment. She is an inspirational, reflective, caring practitioner.

I owe a great deal to my dear friend Val Stothard for reading and rereading drafts of this book and for making a significant contribution towards the section on challenging behaviour. Val has been a source of inspiration and wisdom over many years and I am exceedingly grateful for her friendship, inspiration and support.

Special thanks go to Rebecca O'Sullivan who produced the artwork for this book.

Thanks also go to Jenny Terry, an amazing, playful practitioner and friend, whose reflective nature and helpful comments have helped to guide my thinking over the many years.

Thanks to Penny Pell for her down-to-earth advice and comments. She always manages to see the funny side of life and this helps to keep my feet on the ground whenever I got bogged down with theory and philosophy.

I extend much gratitude to Dave Hewett, who, some five years ago, challenged me to shed light on playful interactive processes embedded within interactive music. This proved to be the catalyst and inspiration for Masters research and, subsequently, for this book. Dave continues to be an accessible beacon of light for practitioners working in the field of special needs.

I applaud David Reid (head teacher) for his unwavering dedication to the young people in his care. His creative, insightful leadership makes a difference to all who are lucky enough to walk his way. I am also especially grateful to him and to deputy head Ginny Marshall for encouraging my professional development, which led to a postgraduate diploma in play therapy.

I honour Wendy Prevezer, who, over 20 years ago, embedded within me an inspiration and a desire for a work that was to become such a huge part of my life.

Thanks to Rachel Gardner for her interest in this work and for reading and commenting on an earlier draft.

Thank you Rod Parker Rees for your encouragement and for kindly sharing your knowledge and expertise throughout my academic journey and beyond.

Thanks to Coleen Jackson, my tutor at the University of Chichester.

I give a special mention to the research participants (MA Ed 2007) who so willingly shared their views and insights; they were amazing, wonderfully different and a joy to work with.

I am grateful to Hannah Foster for her interest in this work and for helping me to produce the music score for this book.

Thanks to Laura Blake for her insightful comments on and contribution to the final chapter.

I applaud, very loudly, the children with whom I have worked over many years. In truth, they have taught me all I know in real terms. Practitioners take note: enter a child's world, actively listen and follow their lead – they are surprising and wonderful human beings!

Thanks be to God.

Part 1

Playfulness: theory and practice

Chapter 1

Introduction

This book is essentially about playfulness and the importance of a practitioner's interactive style when communicating with people with profound and multiple or severe learning difficulties (PMLD/SLD) and those with autism spectrum disorder (ASD). It is also a practical guide for creative interactive work in schools and beyond.

Building on existing work (Corke, 2002), this book adds another layer to an increasing body of literature associated with interactive approaches (Nind and Hewett, 2006). It also draws on research which sought to uncover aspects of practitioner style and competency, within the context of severe learning difficulty (Corke, 2007).

Playfulness is important; it creates an alternative space where emotional, cognitive and social dimensions can be explored and tested. An experimental frame of mind (playing with roles, ideas, words, concepts and objects) proves to be the core component of practitioner playfulness (ibid.). Considering playfulness as experimental, as opposed to amusement and entertainment, raises the possibilities for this forgotten phenomenon. Many practitioners know in their heart the value of playfulness but its value, in educational terms, appears nominal. This book aims to make playfulness widely acceptable, not only in the teaching and learning process in schools but also across a spectrum of adult services caring for people with SLD/PMLD and ASD.

Some readers will want to explore theories linked to practice; they will be interested in the research and how the deductive processes led to claims that playfulness is an 'experimental frame of mind' (ibid.). Most practitioners, however, in my experience, will simply want to buy into, explore, play and experiment with the practical side of this book. Practitioners will deduce whether or not a particular activity works by 'having a go'; they will observe and record outcomes and in so doing draw their own conclusions. Young people who access activities will also be part of this deductive process because, quite simply, if an activity does not 'press their buttons' they will ignore it or signal discontent. If, however, they smile and jiggle, laugh even, and manage to slowly develop their interest and interaction then yes, you will know that in spite of all the research and practice-based theorising, you have found a way to reach, teach and develop the potential of the young people with whom you work and care. At a time when scientific evidence is highlighting the importance of early nurturing experiences (Gerdhardt, 2003) we cannot ignore the centrality and importance of strategies that help to bring pleasure, meaning and coherence to children's lives.

The first chapters of this book offer a blend of theory, philosophy and practical guidance to underpin playful practice. The latter part is dedicated to practical ideas concerned with creative interactions (combining the use of intensive interaction with the arts): interactive music, interactive musical movement, finger dance, story and drama, artwork and reflective circle. Songs, games and activities have been devised primarily for young people with significant intellectual impairment but I want to stress that the application of this developmentally driven work is also very relevant to children in early years education where play and playfulness are seen to be fundamental commitments within the Early Years Foundation Stage (DFE, 2009)

It is always difficult to find key words to represent people when trying to relay a message or storyline. For ease of reading I have used the term PMLD/SLD to refer to people with severe intellectual impairment. I am aware that autism is increasingly viewed as a condition rather than a disorder but I use the term ASD because it is most commonly used and understood at present. The term 'practitioner' is used widely in this book to encompass a wide range of professionals working in education, early years, therapy/clinical services and adult care services, but I also include parents and carers in my thoughts as I write because they are central to a child's well-being. The term 'children' is used widely, but again, as I write I am keeping in mind all those who would benefit from playfulness, and that's a lot of people.

Although this book is largely about practitioner playfulness, an essential thread running alongside this main theme concerns the education, nurture and development of children with PMLD/SLD. It is helpful to facilitate children's access to their innate playfulness because play is central to knowledge acquisition in the foundational stages of learning. As practitioners, it helps to be playful in order to make learning accessible: 'laughter, fun and enjoyment, sometimes being whimsical and nonsensical, are the best contexts for learning' (ibid.: 9).

Throughout the text, I have added speech bubbles containing relevant comments from practitioners. Some of the statements were taken directly from research data (Corke, 2007), some were made by colleagues working with children with PMLD/SLD on a day-to-day basis and other statements arose during in-depth conversations with specialists.

I hope this book encourages you to embrace and 'practise' playfulness in your work and that this helps to enrich the lives of others.

Chapter 2

Context for learning

Knowing, acknowledging and delivering where the child is

Within the field of special needs there are huge variations in abilities and competencies due to each individual's medical or psychological profile. Disordered development, epilepsy, physical or sensory impairment and autism spectrum disorder are just some of the many factors affecting learning. The categorisation of people with cognitive impairment can be problematic and there can be confusion between developmental delay and developmental disorder.

A child who arrives at key developmental milestones in typical order but at a slower rate may be said to be developmentally delayed. Children, on the other hand, with a developmental disorder (atypical) tend to have specific gaps in their profile: some skills may appear appropriate but there will be significant delay in a number of areas. A third group involves children whose difficulties have been acquired after a period of normal development. Here a significant injury to the brain, for example, will impact on skills already developed but also on skill acquisition in the future. These children's profile presents as patchy and they may have to start the learning process again from the very beginning.

Thus, a child may be categorised as having PMLD/SLD but the nature of their impairment is likely to be significantly different from one person to another. Knowing a child's cognitive profile includes consideration of their strengths and difficulties and this is key when deciding on an appropriate style or method of intervention. It is evident that all these children have some measure of difficulty with the challenges involved in social interaction; they often have problems communicating and connecting meaningfully with people in their environment and this can lead to individuals becoming socially adrift and isolated. The pioneering work of Nind and Hewett (1994), based on the detailed and critical learning aspects occurring between infants and caregivers during the first 18 months of life (Kellet and Nind, 2003: 8), has provided a rich landscape of hope for people with PMLD/SLD. There is an ever-increasing body of work supporting the value of intensive interaction and I refer you to the intensive interaction website for more information. You will discover that intensive interaction is embedded in all the creative activities presented in the second half of this book.

Intensive interaction

'Intensive interaction is an approach to teaching the pre-speech fundamentals of communication to children and adults who have severe learning difficulties and/or autism and who are still at an early stage of communication development' (www.intensiveinteraction.co.uk).

In truth, we know that children with PMLD/SLD remain psychologically young throughout their lives. This inevitably has a major impact on their lives and learning ability. The challenge for practitioners to provide a rich and meaningful curriculum is often met with astonishing creativity and enthusiasm. Government demand, however, for goal setting and progression often thwarts practitioners' best efforts because formulaic systems do not necessarily match the child's often uneven profile. The widely used P-level system, for example, contains some phrases and goal-directed sentences that bear little relation to what a child with PMLD/SLD can actually do. There is a sense, too, if I may be so bold as to suggest, that these assessment models are not actually about moving a child on but rather about a need to justify the teachers' own work. I have issues, too, with moderation because practitioners, in my experience, have differing views around a child's level of attainment. Some teachers simply 'mark up' because a child has loosely met a certain criterion and this can leave subsequent teachers with limited room to manoeuvre in terms of quantifiable progression.

We all know that children with PMLD/SLD are likely to have uneven profiles; their learning and progress is less likely to be quantifiable in terms of a hierarchical or linear continuum. So why, I wonder, is this rarely taken into account in government literature? We need, I believe, to create a system that acknowledges children's conditions/disorders, individual medical issues, strengths and real-life possibilities. There are of course positive developments in the area of PMLD/SLD curriculum: 'Routes for Learning' (2006), for example, offers a helpful framework that many practitioners are now adopting but, for me, there is still some way to go in terms of curriculum formation to ensure breadth and depth of experience for our special learners. The National Strategies Early Years Foundation Stage (DFE, 2009) guidance documents present a useful benchmark that could help to steer thinking in the areas of pedagogy and fundamental learning in special schools.

The issue of curriculum formation cannot be fully explored within the remit of this book but I urge those working with government agencies, researchers, academics and, most importantly, practitioners to take up the challenge to change the system.

Practitioners might want to consider perusing developmental assessment tools such as the Hawaii Early Learning Profile (Parks, 1994) to inform their knowledge and understanding. Such profiles track development and offer helpful, finite detail of the complex early learning process in key developmental areas.

The study of infancy and how this relates to children with PMLD/SLD

It is relatively easy to draw parallels between developments in infancy and those with PMLD/SLD: the fundamental nature of pre-verbal experience, dependency on others, sense of vulnerability and fragile autonomy appears equitable. There are, however, many other factors that affect learning for people with PMLD/SLD that need to be taken into account. This said, comparing the levels of competence has, undoubtedly, been helpful because studies of infancy have provided practitioners with enormous insight into the puzzle of social, communication and cognitive development (Stern, 1977, 1985; Schaffer, 1998; Trevarthen, 2002, Reddy and Trevarthen, 2004).

Much of the infant's learning takes place within dynamic social interactions with more able partners. These one-to-one, face-to-face encounters, described by Parker-Rees (2004: 36) as 'the full on, eye-to-eye, soul-to-soul engagement' are often intimate and emotionally intense.

The infant instinctively learns the fundamentals of communication within this emotionally charged environment and an air of playfulness and teasing seeps into the interactive process as the infant grows (Reddy and Trevarthen, 2004). This early intervention model, coupled with an adult's positive encouraging interactive style and active play behaviour, appears to be a major factor in developing and extending skills for people with PMLD/SLD (Corke, 2002; Nind and Hewett, 1994, 2005; Prevezer, 1991, 2000; Hewett, 2006; Sonders, 2003).

That playfulness seeps into the process of engagement is hardly surprising because 'activities which are basically pleasurable are likely to generate feel-good chemicals' (Gerdhart, 2010: 63). The quality of emotional experiences a child receives impacts greatly on how they make use of learning opportunities.

I like Smith's (1995: 19) vision of an interactive scene: he suggests that 'early playfulness is like a symphony or ballet, a choreographed event'.

To illustrate:
Eric and Annie (9 months old) play in a lively way. Eric leads the interaction; he is down on his knees, adjusting his voice so that he sounds like a gentle monster. 'Here I come, here I come', he says as Annie scuttles off. Eric's moves are measured, not too quick, not too slow, and he registers her response all the time. Slowly and carefully he approaches, repeating the 'here I come' phrase. She knows he is coming, gets excited and makes panic-type vocalizations. 'Argh', goes Eric as he gently grabs and cuddles her; laughter bursts ensue and the 'coming-to-get-you' game is repeated.

During this wonderful game I reflected on the process: Eric and Annie's moves were influenced and regulated by each other in amazingly intricate ways. They reinforced each other and both appeared happy and satisfied with the outcome. Fogel (1993) calls joint action relationship experience like this, where spontaneity and creativity blend together, 'co-regulation'. Such interaction, he suggests, 'allows the individual to participate in the discovery of the unknown and the invention of possibilities' (p. 6). As I watched Eric play I deduced an experimental frame of mind in action. Following the playful event, Eric felt a sense of satisfaction; his ideas and playful experimentation were received eagerly and this helped to forge a positive relationship between grandfather and granddaughter. For Annie, too, there was satisfaction, but underlying her satisfaction was the real possibility for social and cognitive growth.

What was Annie learning?

- that playfulness and fun feel good;
- how to enjoy being with another person;
- to 'tune in' emotionally to another person;
- to regulate her behaviour;
- that she has the power to affect her physical and social world;
- that relationships arouse internal feelings;
- a basic understanding of emotions such as joy, fear and surprise;
- to hold in mind knowledge of play routines, rules and outcomes;
- signalling behaviours that will lead to intentional communication: gestures, vocal patterns and words;

- timing;
- cause and effect – when I do this something happens;
- sequencing – the play routine has a beginning, middle and end;
- object permanence – things exist even when out of sight;
- that she is special!

Playful songs and game routines involving burst–pause, tension–expectancy, imitation, physical contact, tuneful rhymes and conversational vocal/physical turn-taking are all commonly used by caregivers during the natural, intuitive parenting process. Parents unwittingly 'teach' infants about their physical and social world in this playful, nurturing environment. Suspense games such as 'here I come – got you' 'peek-a-boo' and 'tickle' ensure the caregiver's playful toolkit is full of surprise, delight and fun. The infant is 'likely to have experienced a dozen or more variations of the peek-a-boo games' during early interactive episodes (Stern, 1985: 106). It is not difficult to visualise the playful ambiance created by caregivers as they actively listen and respond intuitively. Hobson (2002: 43) captures the spirit of this beautifully, describing the playful social life of an eight-month-old infant as being a 'fountain of pleasure, a reservoir of reassurance and a wellspring of mischief'.

To help unlock the potential of these early play experiences, practitioners need to acquaint themselves with the strategies involved in this early interactive play process. Tension–expectancy and burst–pause are central features of play routines.

Tension–expectancy

Tension sensed during early play routines is like suspense – a feeling of uncertainty that may cause a little anxiety (tension) in the short term. Levels of tension will vary depending on the individual and whether or not an outcome is known. There is a sense of drama and anticipation. When the atmosphere created is playful, a child **expects** a pleasurable outcome, albeit one that is 'surprising'. N.B. tension–expectancy games are also known as suspense games or anticipation games.

Burst–pause

Burst – something is happening: a simple song, a physical movement (holding a child while rocking side to side, for example), a tickle or a story line.
Pause created by intentionally stopping – pausing, perhaps dramatically or expectantly. The pause allows a gap – a still moment, a space that enables and encourages a child to slot in a word, vocalisation, movement or gesture.

The mutual interaction generates in the infant a self-experience of very high excitation, full of joy and suspense but, conversely, perhaps tinged with a sense of fear (Stern, 1985: 102). The phenomenon of infant teasing has been highlighted by Reddy and Trevarthen (2004). They consider the instinctive competence of a particular nine-month-old infant and their ability to initiate and sustain a teasing game. During a period of observation, they interpreted the infant's behaviour as recognising the shared understanding required for a give-and-take game. They note progression towards the infant 'playfully and intentionally violating that understanding in order to elicit an emotional reaction from the other person' (Reddy and Trevarthen, 2004: 12).

The infant's growing ability leads to turn-taking; 'they learn about patterns and rules, and become increasingly able to read games' (Scarlet et al., 2005: 48). Gradually infants learn to initiate games of their own and all this leads to a developing capacity for imaginative play.

During these formative years there are noticeable developmental changes as the child's cognitive competence grows. Caregivers play a major role in developing cognition as well as sociability because their actions and 'mediation greatly influences the infant's sense of wonder and avidity for exploration' (Stern, 1985: 103). Again there are parallels to be drawn and lessons to be learnt from the early years. A positive, facilitative environment, where children are encouraged to explore possibilities will help them discover new ways of doing things. Motor skills can be refined, object concept developed and thought processes expanded.

To illustrate:
At 12 months Annie tries things out; she tends to go from one activity to another, using all her senses (vision, audition, olfaction (smell), taste and touch) to experiment and explore. She decides what is successful and rewarding and what is of little interest. In truth, she prefers ornaments and household items to toys and she loves TV remote controls because they have buttons just the right size for her tiny fingers. Despite all the toys and marketing ploys in the world, her own innate curiosity proves to be the key to learning.

There is just one more aspect to this contextual framework (knowing, acknowledging and delivering where the child is) that I would like to add. We now know that warm, nurturing relationships in infancy are crucial to a child's well-being (Gerdhardt, 2003). Positive experiences generate more sophisticated neural networks that help a child develop life skills such as concentration, empathy, understanding and creativity, and as an almost added bonus, the immune system seems to work better (Panksepp, 1998: 249). Negative experiences, on the other hand, affect a child's ability to regulate emotional feelings and behaviour and the possibility for long-term emotional disruption is real and frightening. The fact that early relational poverty affects a child's ability to learn is important. Such information should, at the very least, require us to regularly question our practice to ensure a child's emotional well-being remains at the forefront of our thinking. What and how we do things in the classroom is important.

A child who views a classroom environment as fundamentally friendly is more likely to attend, show interest and actively engage in the learning journey. Conversely, a child who views an environment as cold, uncaring or threatening is likely to switch off, withdraw or behave in unhelpful ways. Playful practitioners improve the quality of provision because they are fun to be with; they experiment with possibilities outside curriculum norms and value the process of encounter. Gerdhardt (2010: 212) states that 'babies are not preparing for school, they are learning about their bodies and their emotions'. This perhaps begs a question: What, in the grand scheme of things, do we think children with PMLD/SLD are preparing for?'

Chapter 3

Theory and definition

Why consider playfulness?

Interest in playfulness can be traced back to the early 1930s when Dewey (1933), an important agent of change in education, explained that playfulness is more important than play. 'The former is an attitude of mind; the latter is a passing outward manifestation of this attitude' (p. 210).

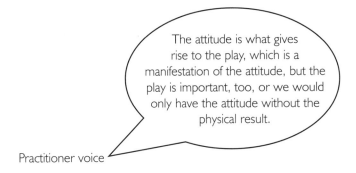

The attitude is what gives rise to the play, which is a manifestation of the attitude, but the play is important, too, or we would only have the attitude without the physical result.

Practitioner voice

Playfulness

Playfulness concerns our internal world – thoughts, feelings and emotions arising as we investigate, explore and experiment with our physical, social and mental worlds.

Play

Play is the tangible, observable manifestation of internal thought processes. Exploring and experimenting take centre stage in self-directed, self-satisfying activities.

Many years later, Lieberman (1977: 6) laid claim to the phrase 'playfulness as an intriguing phenomenon and qualitative ingredient in play'. Playfulness, she explained, 'goes beyond the childhood years . . . it has major implications for child-rearing practices, educational planning, career choices and leisure pursuits' (p. xi). In the 1970s she explored playfulness and its relationship to creativity and imagination. She suggested, 'the spontaneous, joyful, glint-in-the-eye aspects [of playfulness] can be beneficial to stimulating imagination and creativity in the class-room' (p. 133). Over 30 years on, the benefits of playfulness in the teaching and learning process do not appear to have been fully realised. This book is an attempt to redress this and bring forth new and exciting ways to engage children and, in particular, those with PMLD/SLD.

'Playfulness is fundamental to our ability to function within social groups throughout our lives' (Parker-Rees, 1999: 61); it has a powerful role to play in relationships (Mount, 2005) and aids learning because of its inherent links with creativity (Dewey, 1933; Csikszentmihalyi, 1975, 1996; Lieberman, 1977; Parker-Rees, 1999, 2000).

Playfulness involves fun and enjoyment and may be good for our health! Laughter is a natural outcome of playful events and, as Strickland (1993: 22) explains, there are physiological and health benefits of laughter: muscle tension melts as adrenaline, endorphins and enkephalins are released and the body's natural pain-killing chemicals are deployed to create a sense of well-being, which helps to reduce the physical effects of stress.

The National Children's Bureau (2006) refers to play as being central to well-being and demonstrates how play and playfulness can help children 'attain, maintain and retain emotional equilibrium'. Playing, Winnicott (2005) insists, allows the child or adult to be creative and 'it is only in being creative that the individual discovers the self' (p. 54). It seems evident that creativity and playfulness are close cousins! Thus, experimenting playfully with concepts, ideas, words, numbers, thoughts, objects and roles helps children to develop knowledge, imagination and creativity (Corke, 2007).

What is playfulness?

> Playfulness is to do with not being aware of our boundaries or rules or frontiers that can stop your freedom of thought.

Practitioner voice

Playfulness is often linked with the concept of play but this has caused conceptual confusion in terms of unpicking the essence of what appears to be a complicated, multifaceted, feeling phenomenon. Play is viewed as having both positive and negative elements (Scarlet et al., 2005), whereas the perception of playfulness tends to suggest fun, joy and frolicsome abandonment. Theories of play are unlikely to be attributable to a particular event or behaviour. In the same way, playfulness appears singularly indefinable. Glynn and Webster (1992: 84) agree, stating that playfulness exists on numerous levels and is a characteristic of individuals, interpersonal interactions and social systems. Playfulness can be perceived as quiet and intimate, raucous and wild or subtle and humorous. Scarlet et al. (2005: 3) view play as the 'experience of playing' and stress that we should 'consider multiple criteria for defining play rather than settling on one definition alone'. Within the construct of playfulness, a multi-faceted definition appears most likely.

Playfulness, however, as Maxwell *et al.* (2005: 224) suggests, has two faces: 'fun loving and frivolous'. The downside of playfulness is perceived by them as 'the tendency to mess around... live in a fantasy world and waste time on trivial matters'. Paradoxically, this kind of light-hearted, free expressiveness proves central to playfulness in the early years (National Children's Bureau, 2006). While aspects of playfulness can be generalised, there are likely to be discrepancies between ages and contexts, and practitioners working in the field of special education need to find a balance and a compromise that best fits their practice.

Do adults find it easy to be playful? Interestingly, Maxwell *et al.* (2005) found no difference, due to age, of being fun-loving, but there was a degree of difference, due to age, in that older people tended to be less frivolous. Perhaps this is why practitioners sometimes find playfulness difficult – frivolity in adulthood is not necessarily viewed as a good thing. Adults are likely to feel more comfortable when playfulness is linked with humour – the kind of humour that evokes feelings of amusement in others. Morreall (1987) defined a theory of humour and laughter by explaining that 'laughter results from a pleasant psychological shift, whereas humour arises from a pleasant cognitive shift'. This comparison may be particularly significant when considering the cognitive possibilities of people who are functioning at a very low developmental level. Although unlikely to appreciate humour, developmentally, young children may benefit from the pleasant psychological effects caused by playfulness.

Humour

Verbal humour, such as puns, jokes and sarcasm, may not be appropriate for people with delayed or disordered profiles as they require a higher level of cognition and language ability. Visual forms, however, (cartoons, costumes and props) and physical forms, such as slapstick, enhance the playful practitioner's toolkit.

With humour there is a build-up and anticipation, whereas laughter is experienced in the here and now and arises as a spontaneous response to external stimuli. 'Sharing laughter together often serves as a precursor to other forms of social intimacy' and an interesting correlation can be observed between humour and aggression because both can be used to control people (Scarlet *et al.*, 2005: 102).

Playfulness, then, has to be modulated and relevant to context. For example, Annie usually plays chase and tickle games with Aunty Jane but it wouldn't be appropriate for her to do so during Auntie Jane's wedding service or for Annie to try to engage the vicar in playful ways at the same time. Thus, in the act of playfulness, children are learning about boundaries: you can be playful in this or that context or with a certain familiar person but not with another. Children learn, too, about self-regulation because complex second-by-second signals and reciprocal feedback cycles inherent in the play process help them to understand the rules of social engagement. Children learn that this 'move' is OK because it gets a certain response while another move proves less rewarding. Heightened emotional connections, too, seem to have a secondary purpose in playful processes because children learn and experience feelings (sometimes joy, fear, excitement, shock and surprise) within a safe, protected space. We use a child's natural language and become childlike in order to communicate meaning and understanding and this, in turn, helps to clarify the rules of social engagement. Playfulness is not just fun for fun's sake, there is so much more going on.

I have endeavoured to encapsulate the stages of playfulness in a progressive chart to offer some key markers for practitioners who may be involved in curriculum planning. I have not attempted, however, to connect play and playfulness within a precise developmental framework because playfulness with children with PMLD/SLD can be free-wheeling and variable. The play/playfulness scale, therefore, is not a set menu but, rather, a movable feast.

Play/playfulness scale	
Social	**Cognitive**
Social awakening – playing with aural and motor movements, crying. Facial expressions and reflexive vocal sounds. Use sense of smell.	Sensory awakening – developing awareness of own body sensations in relation to the environment.
Shows signs of enjoyment when caregiver mirrors actions – two-way playful exchanges.	Reflexive play – accidental discovery of physical world – some tracking.
Vocal play and vocal dialogues.	Visual play – observation of objects – mobiles, locating, tracking.
Interactive play – adults exaggerated vocal/tactile playfulness cause smiles and giggles.	Sensory play – touching/mouthing objects, grasp development.
Physical play – responds with smiles and giggles to hugging, tickling, swinging, bouncing.	Discovery play – growing awareness that actions can affect immediate environment.
Repetitive play routines – burst–pause and tension–expectancy games – repetition important.	Cause-and-effect play – grasp and release – pushing, pulling and investigating in close proximity to objects.
Imitative play – copies others actions and shows delight at results, e.g. clapping, jumping and pointing.	Physical play – refining gross and fine motor control. Gaining control over physical world.
Rough-and-tumble play – co-active physical frolicking and exaggerated playfulness.	Intentional play – plays and discriminates between favourite objects and shows preferences. Makes choices.
Parallel play – play alongside peers but not actually engaged with or in the same mindset of a game.	Exploratory play – solitary investigation and experimentation. Developing object concept and object permanence (objects exist out of sight).
Social play – shared attention to objects, people and games.	Peer play – child copies other children's moves.
Co-operative play – playing with peers with a shared understanding of rules and the game plan.	Symbolic play – child uses toys and objects to represent real objects and the actions associated with them.
Pretend play – children take on roles and enjoy adults watching and reinforcing play ideas.	Construction play – making things, building towers, construction kits.
Imaginative play – make-believe.	
Dramatic play – objects and props influence play ideas and themes when playing with others.	

Chapter 4

Steps to playfulness

Practitioner/process

The practitioner

This section relates to practitioner styles and interactive play competencies when communicating and relating with people with PMLD/SLD.

Human connectedness is complex; it involves enormous sensitivity, regulation and attunement. The role of the practitioner in the communication and play process is of primary importance. An 'open' inviting presence and playful facilitation encourages a child to enter the learning arena with a positive frame of mind. Nind and Hewett (2005: 6) agree; they highlight the value of 'process-centred' teaching and suggest that 'interactive play has a crucial role in ongoing development'. Their research shows that playful work is more enjoyable and effective for PMLD/SLD learners. They stress, too, the importance of person-centred teaching styles because this, in their experience, helps practitioners to become more interesting and accessible to learners. This view is shared by Bruner (1990) who recognised the crucial role of interactive play for the development of social and cognitive abilities.

Non-verbal communication – tone of voice (intonation), warmth, sensitive touch, facial expression and movement – all relay messages, and children are often very good at 'reading' whether our intention is genuine or not. 'The possession of the attitude that you are prepared to be playful' is seen to be especially important (Nind and Hewett 2005: 91). In the two-way playful process, arousal modulation, too, is important because 'the central nervous system has a need or drive to keep arousal at an optimum level'; too much or too little stimulation causes disturbance in well-being (National Children's Bureau, 2006).

The practitioner, then, needs to get the balance right: too much control and play is not playful or fun, too little control and it can lead to confusion and chaos. Importantly, the adult needs to regulate his/her own behaviour and this then becomes part of learning for the child. Adult regulation teaches children how to regulate behaviour: children need to know when to stop and we have a responsibility to teach them by example (see Figure 4.1).

Lieberman (1977) identified cognitive spontaneity as a key feature of playfulness. Spontaneity is relatively easy to achieve in childhood but more difficult in later years because adults tend to be self-questioning and reserved (Maslow, 1987: 65). Discussing self-acceptance and spontaneity with insightful flair, Maslow likens the movements of a dancer, 'spontaneous, fluid, automatically responsive to the rhythm of the music', as being indicative of self-forgetfulness. The natural, interactive process between child and practitioner can be reflected within Maslow's text:

Most will try, will be directed, self controlled, and purposeful, will listen to the rhythm of the music *(child),* and by a conscious act of choice fall in with it *(the interaction)* ... They will never enjoy dancing *(the interaction)* as a profound experience of self forgetfulness and voluntary renunciation of control unless they finally transcend trying and become spontaneous.

(p. 65)

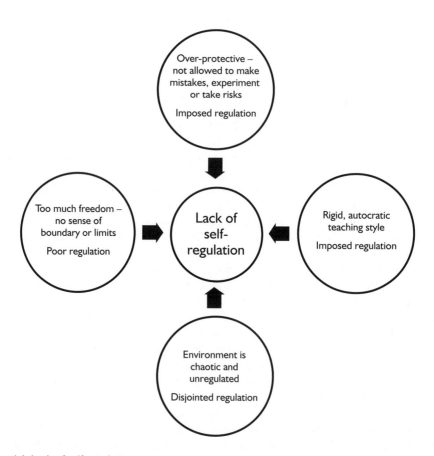

Figure 4.1 Lack of self-regulation

Leiberman (1977: 149) suggests 'the playing child and the playing adult may become more alike' and this indicates harmonious possibilities for attunement and relationship building. 'Both partners feel free to contribute to the process and each respect the others right to do so' (Fogel, 1993: 41). When we adopt a playful style we become more childlike but we are not childish because we retain our adult status and sensibility and this helps to 'hold' the child in a safe place.

The practitioner is tentative yet earnest as he or she seeks entry to the fragile interpersonal world of a child with PMLD/SLD.

To illustrate:

Tom is a nine-year-old child with PMLD.

Stage 1 – Tom and I lie together in close proximity on a floor mat. I mirror his movement to let him know that I am eager to relate and connect to him in a way that he can understand. I regulate my breathing to mirror his in an attempt to enhance our attunement. We are in a pleasant state for several minutes, meeting and greeting with fleeting and sometimes sustained eye contact.

Stage 2 – After a while I take a risk and gently introduce a playful vocal game: 'dum dee dum dee dum'. Initially, I simply say the words tunefully to introduce the game. I am also assessing his readiness to proceed. Not that I have a predetermined plan here, rather I am sensing and playing with the process as I go along. I tentatively add a gentle rhythmic tapping movement onto his chest to accompany the vocal game. I monitor his second-by-second responses: the final 'dum' becomes a flat hand jiggle. I can tell from his eyes (gleaming and alert) that he is enjoying the experience. I decide to go further and play with the intonation of the words, adding a gasping pause before the more purposeful jiggling tickle, at the end of the phrase, where a flat hand is placed on his chest. It elicits a smile and then a giggle. The game is repeated three times before Tom's arousal level drops. He is unable or unwilling to sustain attention and his interest wanes. It is vital here to read Tom's cues – too much stimulation could prove hurtful and damaging to our relationship. We return to a simple, quiet, comfortable state. After about two minutes Tom makes a loud vocal sound, which I mirror but I also add intention to his vocal sound by repeating the dum dee dum game. He smiles as I begin, and this lets me know that it's OK to continue. Had he grimaced, turned away or offered any other negative signal, I would have stopped and returned to our gentle child-led interaction.

Once entrenched in an intimate two-way process, playfulness moves the interaction to another level because as Mount (2005: 5) explains, playfulness 'may be one way that individuals manage emotional closeness to a partner'. As practitioners, if we ignore variability and playful creativity we risk missing 'the core of the process and the excitement that keeps us involved' (Fogel, 1993: 41). The word 'co-regulation' has been used to describe successful interaction. Shaped by both parties; there is equality – no sense of control and the outcome is unpredictable at the outset. Reddy and Trevarthen (2004) explain the importance of engagement and participation in this intimate two-way process. Parental play styles, 'attributes and personality traits influence children's tendency toward playfulness' and creativity (Smith, 1995: 19).

During Intensive Interaction, when attunement is established, a state of blissful flow is achieved. Corresponding with the natural parenting model, playfulness and creativity mingle within the process and this helps to break down barriers, build trust and develop communication skills.

Intentionality

Intentionality is about making an assumption that a child's non-intentional action, vocalisation or movement is an attempt to communicate meaning (request or comment). We add intention to a child's action, vocalisation or movement by responding as if it were a request or comment and by acknowledging this with actions or words to reinforce and encourage a child to learn about the message-carrying possibilities of their movements, gestures and vocalisations.

The playful practitioner shows a real interest in the child and values every aspect of their communication; He/she challenges them to be creative and to explore new ideas by teasing and cajoling while also paying attention to arousal modulation according to a child's response. The child's interest remains central but both take risks and the practitioner gives abundant positive feedback to encourage and maintain a sense of well-being (Figure 4.2).

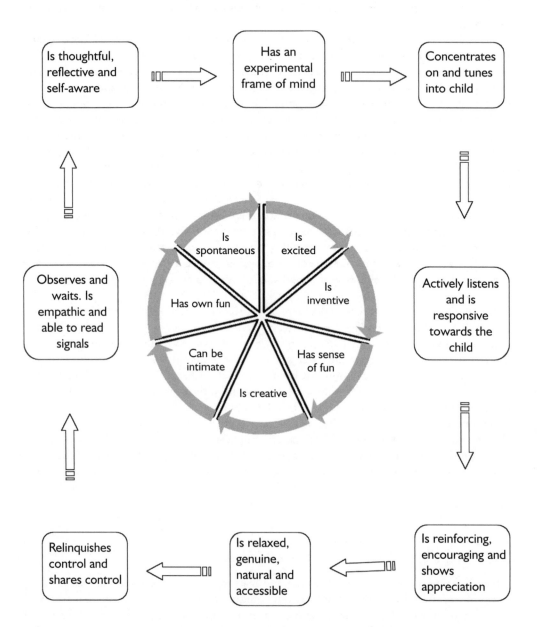

Figure 4.2 The playful practitioner

In 'special' educational settings we need to work from the child's frame of reference, from their agenda. Start from where the child is. There is nothing new in this idea (practitioners have been saying this for years) but, put simply, *we do not do this*. Instead we work largely within frameworks and agendas set by 'higher' powers. We attempt to set goals, track progress and deliver a curriculum that often loses sight of the unique and special person in our care. It is, I believe, our mindset and not our skilfulness that makes a difference to children.

> This does not mean pushing children too far or too fast but instead meeting children where they are; showing them the next open door, and helping them to walk through it. It means being a partner with children, enjoying with them the power of their curiosity and the thrill of finding out what they can do.
>
> (DFE, 2009: 22)

Within interactive approaches, the process, rather than the product, is the central feature, but this perhaps tells only half the story. While the process, as many of us believe, should remain child-centred, there is also a need to create a safe, contained environment to support a child's learning journey. In education, too, there is a need to evidence, celebrate and show off children's work and achievements. What remains crucial involves the way activities and tasks are presented to a child. Learning needs to be interesting and engaging and activities are improved when planned with the capability of learners in mind. Each individual child's strengths and difficulties should be at the heart of our thinking when planning to ensure tasks are within a child's reach – cognitively low enough to acknowledge their skill but high enough to challenge them to move forward and reach their full potential. The balance is not always easy to achieve because children with PMLD/SLD do not progress neatly along the cognitive continuum; rather they tend to have an uneven skill profile and many other factors that impinge on learning. Coupled with this, our knowledge of how to refine and deliver a child-centred, broad and balanced curriculum at a fundamental level is sometimes inadequate and hampered further by 'outside' demand and expectation.

At 12 months my granddaughter is teaching me – she is the choreographer directing and developing our social entwinement. When I introduce a playful game her subtle responses and social signals guide the process and inform my moves. This co-active process proves fundamental to the success of our playful endeavour. I do not dominate the space or place unrealistic goals in her way; rather, we simply meander and merge together. I am witness, container and positive reinforcer, and all this enables her, quite unconsciously, to develop social and cognitive competence.

Is playfulness a teaching technique? For sure it can be used to connect with difficult-to-reach children, those with learning and language difficulties and those with significant cognitive impairment. The fact that playfulness is largely a frame of mind, however, suggests that the practitioner, as well as the environment, needs to change in order to create a learning-rich environment where positive, nurturing two-way interaction becomes part of the daily norm.

Earlier in the text I quoted Smith (1995: 19), whose vision of an interactive scene suggested the possibility of a choreographed event. I ask myself a question: 'Who is the choreographer?' Is it practitioner or the child? In the grand scheme of things, and considering the lessons learned from intensive interaction, I think the practitioner and child take it in turns. The adult 'holds' and contains the interaction so that it is safe for the child to lead. Herein may lay the heart and dynamic of shaping interactive learning and playfulness. Perhaps the teacher should consider themselves as the choreographer, designing learning sequences for children by considering what a child can do, what they can nearly do and what they can do with minimal support. This notion bears resemblance to Bruner's (1982) 'scaffolding', wherein a framework of support enables a child to successfully complete a task with a little help. When scaffolding is used, in effect the child is practising the skill at first and then the adult slowly removes the support as knowledge grows. Scaffolding works well as long as the scaffold is removed 'piece by piece' in a relatively short space of time. If a child requires support for several weeks, the activity is likely to be beyond their capability, and further refinement is required and even smaller steps put in place. Scaffolding provides an ongoing framework for building up and extending skills, but I want to reiterate that the learning activity needs to be within the capabilities of the child.

Cues

Naturally occurring day-to-day routines and activities provide observable cues for children. For example, it's time for dinner and I know this because I can smell chips and the dinner trolley arrives (olfactory and visual/sound cues), or I feel a tap on my chest and I know it's time for the toilet (touch cue). If I were to stand up or sit down, this too would offer a natural visual cue.

Prompts

Physical, verbal and gestural prompts are used to instruct, guide and direct a specific action. While prompts are often an essential part of the learning process they can be unhelpful because there can be a tendency to use prompting in 'an intrusive, controlling manner, which undermines the shared, reciprocal nature of social interaction' (Goold and Hummell, 1993: 25). Hand-under-hand and sensitive elbow prompts are often a good place to start when using a prompt with a child with SLD/PMLD. Prompts need to be phased out over time to aid learning.

Reddy and Trevarthen (2004: 12) offer helpful insights regarding learning environments: if we observe and 'teach' the interpersonal world of a child from outside, then our approach tends towards 'the imparting of experience by instruction'. If, however, we observe and respond within engagement, then this, in itself, 'necessitates the acknowledgement of the emotionally involved agency of both partners, teacher and learner, who can easily swap roles'. Failure to engage, he further suggests, 'creates a 'sterile and mechanistic understanding of human mental and emotional development' (p. 12). An opportunity to transform knowledge into meaning can be hampered because playful experimentation is limited by the rigidity of a prescriptive model. When a learning environment becomes mechanical and narrow, creativity is squashed.

My quite recent journey into grannyhood has taught me a great deal about early play and interaction. I now understand and agree completely with Reddy and Trevarthen's (2004) suggestion regarding the importance of actual engagement over abstracted observation in gaining psychological knowledge about others. What 'you' and 'your' partner feel during inter-action is difficult to measure in concrete terms.

Sharon (1987: 44), presenting Feuerstein's work, explains how positive 'child adult interac-tions construct children's thinking and behaviour'. Feelings of worth and acceptance are 'brought about by unconditional acceptance, a reduction of anxiety and close supportive rela-tionships' (p. 271). Working within each child's 'zone of proximal development' (Vygotsky, 1978) ensures learning tasks are presented at an appropriate, accessible level. In a similar way to scaffolding, children are challenged to move forward and are offered facilitative support from a more able partner and this helps them to work towards the next developmental mile-stone. The environment created is safe, fun-filled and, as far as possible, 'failure free', leaving a child with an overriding feeling of success.

Zone of proximal development
(Vygotsky 1978)

The 'space' between what a child can do alone and what a child can do when collabo-rating through an adult's active facilitation.

Thus attention to the environment is important. As an educator you may have a goal in mind but you need to remember that a child can get to that goal in lots of different ways. In essence, you can plan where to go but not how you are going to get there. Children find different learning routes and take different amounts of time to achieve a goal. There is a legitimate period of time when an activity has to be child-led; stepping in too early can destroy confi-dence and lead to a child giving up. Self-directed play, in the facilitative company of a more able partner, helps to foster learning and pride in achievements.

To illustrate:
A recent play episode with Annie (12 months) offered a timely reminder that goal setting can be problematic. I had bought a set of stacking pots and a four-piece inset shape puzzle. I had imagined (my goal) that I would stack the pots and that she would bash them down – great fun! The inset puzzle was slightly beyond her level but, again, I imagined that she might at least take the puzzle pieces out. Annie was having none of this. Instead she took great delight in putting the puzzle pieces in a pot and began to shake it vigorously until they jumped out. We laughed out loud together.

The benefit of practitioners being playful, in the sense of fun-loving, is not that it directly causes learning but that it provides a positive, contextual framework to encourage the devel-opment of cognition and sociability. Nind and Hewett (2005: 73) see 'enjoyment, fun and playfulness as powerful motivators in learning'. This idea is reinforced by Bruner (2006: 64) who insists 'a little playfulness is a powerful aid to learning and problem-solving'.

It is worth mentioning that a child with ASD, who's thinking will be more inflexible, may feel comfortable working within a more rigid framework. This does not mean, however, that children with ASD only work within rigid frameworks. Not at all. My experience tells me that so long as there are visual cues, a routine is established and boundaries are clarified, then flexible, free-flowing activities can be tolerated and enjoyed.

Playfulness, then, is about experimenting. The child is freewheeling and trying things out and the adult is open to the possibilities in the here and now. Cajoling, teasing and taking risks are testimony to practitioner playfulness in action. The experimental mind explores different moves but remains flexible enough to move back and forth in order to stay with the child.

Children are all different, observe them in play and use their ideas and special interests as a gateway to learning new skills.

To illustrate:

Steven is a nine-year-old lad with PMLD. He has global development delay, marked visual impairment and severe epilepsy. Steven spends much of his day in a wheelchair. He rarely uses his (often splinted) hands to access equipment and I have never seen him smile.

During interactive music, Steven sat quietly; he heard the songs and occasionally moved his head, seemingly in response, but it was difficult to assess whether this was a reflexive response or interest in, or reaction to, sensory stimuli. On one particular occasion I introduced a 'seaside' prop (blue milk-bottle tops threaded together to form a large circle and draped with white and blue florist ribbons) and this seemed to catch Steven's attention. I knew this because there were subtle changes in his facial expression and his eyes became alert.

The process

1. The activity was offered at a level suitable for Steven (slightly above his head, within his visual field). He watched the ribbons.
2. We gave him ample time to orientate his eyes.
3. We were open to the possibility that he would do more.
4. We gave him more time because there was a marked improvement in his visual interest.
5. Slowly and carefully, we moved the prop (up, down, side to side) to further assess his interest and to encourage tracking.
6. We tentatively facilitated tactile access by using a hand–under–hand prompt.
7. We continued to use a sensitive and mostly a still hand–under–hand prompt just long enough for him to grasp independently.
8. We willed him to hold on – he slowly moved his arms up and down, eliciting a sound from the tops.
9. We were patient and gave him more time – we used no spoken language.
10. We enabled Steven to take control of his own learning.
11. After five minutes of sustained interest he drew the bottles to his mouth, and for a minute or two he used his mouth to explore. Ureka! A first for Steven.

It had taken a period of extended focus and attention, on our part, to enable Steven to be able to use his hands and mouth for independent sensory exploration. Was I being playful? In terms of environment I would say yes: we were using a playful song, and as practitioners we were open to possibilities and actively encouraged playful responses from the children. In terms of my experimental frame of mind, yes again, because we had no idea that Steven would progress in this way. I was experimenting with subtle movements, deciding whether or not to use spoken language, whether or not to continue to sing, trying out different positions for the seaside ring and so on. Was Steven being playful? Yes, he was experimenting with an object, taking a risk, trying things out and enjoying the process.

This was a truly wonderful moment for all involved but it does raise the question regarding group work and how to meet individual needs in a group setting. Teamwork is essential and this will be discussed in Part 2 of this book.

Practitioner's steps to playfulness

Firstly, there is an intention: a genuine, earnest desire to engage; eyes are wide open and exaggerated body, facial and vocal expressiveness are used to interest and engage a partner. Attention is paid to proximity and positioning to ensure possibilities for eye-to-eye contact and there is no sense of invasion in this early stage, simply intricate two-way signals of arousal and approval or disapproval. Reaction and co-regulated responses create feedback cycles and this helps to generate reciprocity because both partners share a willingness to engage and contribute equally to the ongoing play process. The use of 'parentese' brings an affirming, experimental voice into play; intentional pauses help to build tension and eye contact becomes sustained as emotional attunement and co-regulation are achieved.

A continued barrage of subtle signalling behaviours and positive responses lead to repeats. There is constant readjustment according to the child's moves and level of arousal. The practitioner, being ever attentive to the child, facilitates further experimentation by trying out various playful moves but remains sensitive all the time to the child's needs and responses (Figure 4.3).

Motherese/parentese

Infant-directed speech, often known as 'motherese' or 'parentese', is a universal, exaggerated speaking style that is vowel-drenched and playful. The rich and varied acoustical stimulation contained in this speaking style has emotional overtones that help to engage infants.

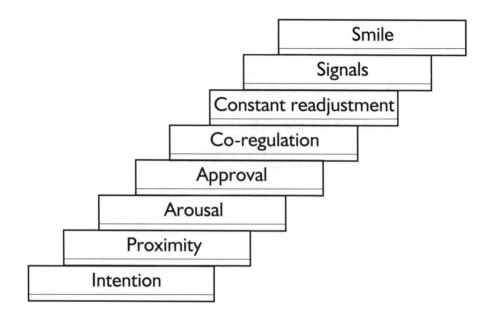

Figure 4.3 Steps to Playfulness

Chapter 5

The tools of playful practice
Experimental frame of mind, voice, body language, touch, modulation, flexibility, fun, flow and creativity

Playfulness is not a technique, more an attitude of mind, but this attitude can be used as a teaching tool. This next section considers the mechanics, the core components, of a playful activity.

> As an experimenter you are collating information from previous experiments (trials). You have a hypothesis but have to run trials to confirm your theory.

Practitioner voice

Experimental frame of mind

'Experimental' is a term usually associated with science: investigations, making predictions and processing data. In a similar way, social interaction requires a certain amount of investigation; we experiment with various verbal and non-verbal signals as we make predictions about our partner's intentions and second-guess their feelings. We then store this information in our brains to inform the ongoing development of a relationship. People experiment with their voice, body language and facial expression in all kinds of ways and in all kinds of situations.

We can try something new. Experimenting with a word, sound or facial expression; exploring possibilities within a play routine; or predicting outcomes during anticipation games all bear witness to experimental thought in action. Reflecting on the variety of experimental facial, body and vocal expressions and the theatrical, experimental nature of game-play, it is perhaps not surprising that playful practitioners seem to possess an experimental frame of mind.

To illustrate:
During interactive music I am presenting a tambourine while Jonny sits making no attempt to engage with me or reach towards the tambourine. It is as if I were not there. My experimental mind activates and I begin to think of playful ways to engage him. My movements become exaggerated – the tambourine goes up, up, up and down. There is a flicker of interest from

Jonny. My experimental mind collates this information and I try again (trials). I hypothesise that if I offer a repeated pattern of actions he will respond a little more. On the next round I note a definite interest which confirms my theory, but then Jonny averts his eyes and leans forward. I have to think again. Importantly I am flexible enough to go with the flow. I repeat the tambourine up, up, up game, using exaggerated speech, but, to acknowledge his downward posture, I drop the tambourine to the floor with a loud crash saying 'down, down, down...crash!' Again I am experimenting. Will he like this or not? Yes, his attention is gained and he shows his pleasure by laughing.

The possibility here for failure was ever-present – the crash may have startled Jonny. I may have been modelling 'inappropriate' behaviour, and so on. An experimental mind, then, is all about pushing boundaries and taking risks; thinking things through on the spot and being flexible enough to go with the child's flow. The game was repeated and ended when Jonny's arousal level dropped.

I think the notion of trial and error comes under this experimental heading. Trial and error requires confidence and self-belief since with error there is a risk of failure. Some people find it easier to follow set rules where they feel safe, but unless practitioners are willing to try and fail, adapt their approach and try again they might miss the opportunity to change a child's life. Trial and error, too, can be used to find out new knowledge about a child – what might happen if I do this or that. Again there is a need to be sensitive, to take into account the child's personality and responses. A child needs to be able to trust your judgement; thus, while trial and error is valuable, risk-taking needs to be subtle and measured towards the child's ability. Using sarcasm, for example, is inappropriate with 'our' children as it holds possibilities of seriously damaging a child's self-esteem.

The voice

The expressive and variable possibilities of the human voice are prolific: practitioners often use their voice with multifaceted magnificence to enhance the social play space. Vocal sounds provide a particularly flexible and expressive medium for highly attuned interactions (Parker-Rees, 2007). A playful, experimental voice uses tones that are vowel-drenched, high, low and dynamically interesting, and this exaggerated expressiveness allows the vocal features of a giant, witch or monster to come out to play. Conversely, reflecting a little of the intimate nature of playfulness, quiet sounds and whispers are, at times, likely to permeate the play space.

Singing, and infant-directed speech with variable and often high-pitched tones appears central in the early developmental process. Parents intuitively use vocal play and lullabies to calm and connect emotionally with their infant. Speech and song are interwoven into close, nurturing moments to facilitate growing competencies in vocal play, and this, in turn, helps to sow the foundations for early speech development. Songs, music and vocal playfulness appear central to the well-being of children with PMLD/SLD (Ockleford, 2008).

Tone of voice is important because tones can be laden with emotional overtones and different tones hold possibilities to affirm or condemn. Vocal tone may offer warmth and support or cause shock and fear. Clearly, the way we speak and relate to children is significant.

Different adults bring different qualities into play. Someone may be loud and boisterous or quiet and reserved. Each can be playful and bring a different aspect into play. A child learns how to respond and how to interact in different circumstances. They learn to modulate their own play activities.

Practitioner voice

Body language

Body language is a form of non-verbal communication that puts across to a partner your level of 'openness' and interest in them. Natural gestures, movements, posture and facial expressions all convey a message; sometimes consciously but unconsciously too. The two-way signalling system observable during infant–caregiver interaction is testimony to the power of interactive body language. One partner increases a smile's intensity, eliciting an even bigger smile from the other partner, which ups the level yet again, and a positive feedback spiral ensues (Stern 1985: 102).

Practitioners often use their whole body in exaggerated experimental ways during playful exchanges: there can be elements of pretence, clowning and extraordinary facial expressions, gentle head nods, smiles and raised eyebrows. Practitioners who are open to engagement intensely watch the child looking for signals of arousal and approval as they experiment with discreet or extreme behaviours that are likely to be outside regular, day-to-day, interactive exchanges. Body language is powerful; it indicates how you feel about a child and how a child is feeling about you.

Some children with PMLD/SLD may have difficulty learning the message-carrying value of body language. Consider gestures, for example: a hand held out to indicate 'give', finger-on-lip gesture to indicate 'shush', or hand waves to symbolise 'hello' or 'goodbye'. Children with PMLD/SLD may not instantly recognise these gestures as having a communicative intent. Many children, on the other hand, in my experience, appear to have an innate sense and ability to 'read' body language and/or the emotional connotation within an exchange. They know when a partner is genuinely seeking engagement or simply attempting to connect without a real desire to engage meaningfully. Copying a child's moves, for example, during intensive interaction, without an intention to engage emotionally, is rarely successful for either partner.

Touch

Touch and physical contact are often taboo subjects, but this is somewhat nonsensical because touch offers the first and most basic means of communication. Touch is fundamental to well-being and, where there is significant intellectual or sensory impairment, is likely to be the most important and necessary aspect of communication.

Interactive games that engage and delight infants often involve physical moves and an exchange of touch between communicative partners (Finnegan 2002). Touch, too, is used to confirm intention, offer comfort, console, reassure and motivate. Practitioners naturally experiment with touch in a multitude of different ways in playful situations (Corke, 2007). Pushing, pulling, tickling, poking, jiggling and hugging are just some of the physical actions observable during the interactive play process.

McLinden and McCall (2002: 98) explain that it can be argued that 'of all modalities that are used in communication . . . touch is the most intimate' and possibly the most powerful, but touching children can involve risk. Huss (1977: 305) explained that this is because touch is a non-verbal communication that can be misinterpreted by both parties involved, resulting in a sense of inappropriateness and embarrassment.

Practitioner need to be mindful because 'touch can all too easily become an autocratic controlling force that may promote passivity, override initiated behaviour, and prohibit active participation' (Goold and Hummell, 1993: 14).

Thoughtfulness and complete sensitivity towards the child is paramount and an individual's personal space should not be invaded without permission. As practitioners we need to be thoroughly aware of the moment-by-moment messages we give to children; they are likely to be able to read negativity in an instant. Thus while it is important to actively listen to a child's body language signals, we should also pay attention to our own. A gentle reassuring voice helps.

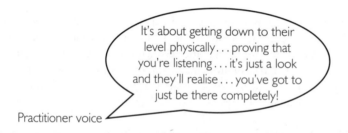

It's about getting down to their level physically . . . proving that you're listening . . . it's just a look and they'll realise . . . you've got to just be there completely!

Practitioner voice

Flow

Joining a child in their world, shelving adult inhibitions and going with the flow creates a unique social space. Playful, creative interactions can be co-created when both partners are open; they go with the flow and each shows a willingness to be shaped by the other (Fogel, 1993: 31). A sense of self-forgetfulness during playful processes can ensue as each partner strives to adjust their physical and emotional state in order to 'take in' the other person. Going with the flow of an interaction in search of optimal experience holds the possibility of lifting the course of an interaction to a different level (Csikszentmihalyi, 1975: 69).

I see flow and tuning in as being fairly similar. I recall, for example, a particular special moment while sitting with my two-month-old granddaughter: we gazed into each other's eyes for what seemed like an eternity; I was mentally inside her and she in me; we were falling in love. This is perhaps the tip of the tuning-in iceberg since, naturally, I do not fall in love with other children in quite the same way. Yet, so often, a positive emotional connection is made and a sense of fondness and mutual regard is realised within this 'forget about everything else around you' tuning-in process.

People become so involved in what they are doing that the activity becomes spontaneous, almost automatic; they stop being aware of themselves as separate from the actions they are performing.

(Csikszentmihalyi, 1975: 53)

Modulation

Practitioners open up a box of social delights when they embrace and deliver sessions incorporating playfulness but this is only half the story. Attention to modulation appears to be paramount because while playfulness can give you a feel-good factor, too much playfulness can be exhausting and over-stimulating to the point where the social engagement becomes uncomfortable.

Playfulness can generate confidence because it allows practitioners to experiment with their face, voice and body in expressive, extreme forms. There are whispers and shouts, tickles, cuddles and grabbing; monster faces, wide-open mouths, steely stares, smiles and laughter. While these extreme human behaviours could serve to foster over-excitement and bedlam, modulation serves to create a boundary between total freedom and the possibility of chaos arising from over-stimulation. This balance helps to keep the space safe and creates a feeling of security for all. Balance, however, is not always easy to achieve and we do need to be aware that different children have different arousal systems. My best advice for creative interactive events is to keep the environment relatively structured so that you can embrace flexibility whole-heartedly within the process. The flexibility bit is really important because although children require boundaries to feel safe and nurtured, boundaries that are too rigid create a culture of control and this can be damaging both educationally and emotionally.

> Modulation is all part of social learning: knowing when to calm, how to self-regulate excitement and when to stop. You can have more fun when an adult knows they can regulate their behaviour in order to bring back calm and order.

Practitioner voice

Playfulness can help 'people know themselves and others' (Cases, 2003: 27), but tolerable levels of play between individuals may depend upon how well each knows the other. Over-zealous practitioners could prove a potential threat to a child; thus care and sensitivity are required to establish trust. The adult's level of sensitivity, open interactive style and respectful attitude are central.

While aspects of playfulness can be generalised, there are likely to be discrepancies between ages and contexts, and practitioners working in the field of special needs probably need to find a balance and compromise that best fits their practice. It seems likely that in mainstream education the use of playfulness relates to context. In a structured classroom the use of play-fulness is likely to be limited, whereas in more freewheeling sessions, such as in a soft-play area or playground, playfulness is likely to dominate. Humour, fun and playfulness, however, remain important in the classroom as they can inform children that you are enjoying being there with them. Playfulness, too, can be helpful when attempting to manage challenging situations because, when used appropriately, it can distract and defuse negative issues. Challenging behaviour is discussed further in Chapter 5.

Just free to explore the different possibilities, like without rules, and finding out what excites a child.

Practitioner voice

Flexibility

A playful practitioner is flexible and open to using trial and error; they expect the unexpected, lack rigidity and do not always assume or predict an outcome.

The interactive journey has to be undertaken 'with' the child and this means adopting a flexible interactive style, taking on and using the behaviour and mannerisms similar to those naturally occurring in childhood.

Meltz and Lutz (1990: 58) explain how a lack of playfulness may be 'related to a restriction of cognitive flexibility'. This, then, suggests that cognitive flexibility may be a key feature of playfulness. Lieberman's (1977: 23) findings were similar. She used observational studies to explore how children play and this enabled her to define playfulness as physical, social and cognitive spontaneity; manifest joy; and sense of humour. Clearly, playing generates a kind of flexibility and a willingness to explore different ideas in order to find new ways of looking at things.

Fun

Playful practitioners like to have fun; they adopt a particular facilitative style that is open, person-specific and childlike. Fun is concerned with something that produces a sense of satis-faction: there can be amusement, entertainment and enjoyment. Fun, having fun and embracing a sense of fun appear to be at the core of practitioner playfulness. Having fun generates a sense of well-being; it causes a feel-good factor and helps to reduce stress (Maxwell *et al.*, 2005).

The spontaneous and attention-gaining qualities of fun are often used during interactive play. Indeed, playfulness and fun appear intrinsically linked. I smiled during the first episode of ITV's *X Factor* in August 2010 when Cheryl Cole commented positively on a lively solo performance: 'When you're having fun we're having fun'. This rang bells for me in terms of our practice: if we are having fun then our children will have fun too – fun is contagious!

Whether or not having fun can actually keep you young, as a colleague of mine suggested, is debatable.

Creativity

The seeds and benefits of creativity were sown some years ago by Dewey (1933) and later, Csikszentmihalyi (1996: 1), who explained that creativity provides 'a central source of meaning in our lives'. Creativity and playfulness seem intrinsically linked. Take, for example, my own experience when creating a piece of art or a new song: I play with ideas; try this and that; and experiment a little with dark and light 'shades', words and melodies until the outcome feels right. Creativity doesn't just happen – having an experimental frame of mind may, however, guide you in the right direction.

It is important to foster creativity within ourselves and 'our' children. 'Creativity improves a pupil's self-esteem, motivation and achievements' and assists pupils in finding ways to 'cope with challenge and responsibilities, to manage risk and to cope with change and adversity'. In essence 'creativity enriches pupils' lives' (QCA, 2005).

Fogel (1993: 31) insists that creativity should take centre stage and points out that 'the emergence of something novel, something that was not there before' creates within us 'openness to the partner' and a 'willingness to allow events to unfold and to be shaped by the process'.

Csikszentmihalyi (1996) explained how creative people possess contradictory extremes in their personality: they may be introvert but also extrovert; can alternate between playfulness and discipline; may be childish yet full of wisdom, and humble and proud at the same time. Further, Csikszentmihalyi stressed that a willingness to take risks in search of innovation is key; creative people are often passionate about their work. Playing, Winnicott (1971) insists, allows the child or adult to be creative and that 'it is only in being creative that the individual discovers the self' (p. 54). Creativity has much to offer both in terms of pedagogy and personal development.

Chapter 6

Special considerations

Children with learning difficulties often have isolated areas of skill that do not necessarily match up with the stages of normal development. This causes confusion and frustration for those involved in the teaching, learning and assessment process. On top of this, a child's disorder/condition impacts on their ability to learn and develop new skills. The challenge facing practitioners is to work with the child's strengths and difficulties while also rigorously acknowledging the inherent problems created by a child's particular condition or disorder. Learning opportunities need to be personalised to ensure a child reaches their full potential.

Autism spectrum disorder

A range of specific traits have become synonymous with ASD but these vary from person to person, and each individual will react to their disability in their own particular way. Wing (1996) identified a triad of impairments to pinpoint three areas of difficulties: social interaction, communication and imagination. Each child with ASD, however, is unique; their personality and history, as well as the inherent qualities of their condition, affects the way they live their lives and how they relate to others.

What is the triad of impairments?

Difficulties with social interactions – turn-taking, sharing, appropriate interactive behaviour, engaging with others

Difficulties with communication – expressive and receptive language, understanding facial expression, understanding body language

Difficulties with imagination/flexible thinking – imaginary play, making transitions and transferring skills, rigid behaviours

---

Children with ASD have an uneven profile of strengths and weaknesses. Some have severe learning difficulties while others are high-functioning. Frith (2003), Hobson (2002) and Berger (2002) discuss blindness in an attempt to explain the nature of autism: 'Imagine trying to bring up a blind child without realising he or she is blind,' notes Frith (p. 223), and Berger explains: 'If you are born blind and visual energy is not transduced to arouse the visual cortex, then your brain does not know it is supposed to see' (p. 23). People with ASD, like those with blindness, do not know what they don't know. They think and act in different ways because their brain structure is unique and different.

People with ASD often suffer from extreme hypersensivity because they fail to process sensory information effectively. When there is sensitivity, reactions to auditory or visual stimuli can, at best, cause a child to cover their ears and/or cringe away and, at worst, arouse a display of uncontrollable, aggressive behaviour as the child attempts to escape a frightening sensory onslaught. Sensory overload arises when people with ASD fail to process sensory information simultaneously. Some gain satisfaction/information from touch, smell and taste but sensitivities in these areas can also arise and, indeed, some children show a high alert response to even the lightest touch or extreme distaste to certain foods or smells.

Thus the notion of a sensory curriculum for all children with PMLD needs to be considered thoughtfully before delivery. The brain, as Berger (2003: 23) explains, 'only deals with information it receives and is equipped to interpret'. Enter the autism spectrum world of a child tentatively; his/her agenda is different from ours and we need to be aware that he/she may have sensitivities in a variety of cognitive, physiological and emotional areas. Care needs to be taken when using interactive music or the creative arts. Certain sounds, together with the multisensory nature of props, hold the possibility of causing pain and anxiety in some. A practitioner who actively listens and alters the input according to the child's response serves the child well. Children with ASD should not be denied access to playful, interactive arts experiences; they often find music helpful and, most certainly, they like to have fun just like the rest of us!

Children with ASD are capable of attachment and social approach behaviours but communicate on their own terms. They lack empathy, showing little or no desire to please a partner during interaction. Limited eye-to-eye gaze for social signalling, an inability to read social cues and their own poorly developed social-signalling behaviours generally prove to be a recipe for systematic failure and breakdown in social relationships. There is a lack of desire to engage with others in joint attention activities and this invariably impacts on play development. Children with autism rarely 'join in' when others laugh and may have little or no desire to elicit smiles and laughter from others. They do, however, have their own sense of fun and, for the most part, engage very well in playful, interactive game routines.

Sensory impairments – visual/hearing impairments

I cannot claim to know a great deal about the sensory impairments of children who are blind/visually impaired, deaf or hearing impaired but I do have a little experience of working with children in this area. Our role, as far as I can see, is to adjust our approach and behaviour to take into account the child's individual profile. This, together with sensitive engagement enables us to offer an empathic understanding of what their world might be like. I never stop asking myself, 'What does this or that feel like for you?' Try sitting in an assembly with your eyes and/or ears closed; communicate a need without vision or language or let a fellow practitioner move you around with your eyes and ears covered. It's a scary place indeed!

Blind children and those with other sensory impairments have knowledge of the world that is unique and quite different. Management of their physical and social learning environment requires special attention and thoughtfulness. The pace with which activities are delivered needs to be matched to the child's pace and a child who is blind or visually impaired is likely to take much longer to orientate themselves towards the stimuli on offer. Tactile experiences (feeling, moving and touching) are central, and consistent predictable routines will help to build confidence.

Each child with visual impairment has a unique profile and this needs to be taken into account because levels of visual functioning differ and can be variable from child to child. Sensory-impaired children enjoy playfulness but sensitivity and attention to detail is important in order to get the level of intervention right. It is wise to avoid startling or frightening a child who is blind/visually impaired during creative interactive play processes by making loud noises or sudden moves without prior warning. Altogether, reflect and modify according to need.

Profound and multiple learning difficulties

Children with PMLD have complex needs. Their responses can be affected by medication, learned passivity, stereotyped behaviours and a variety of factors linked to individual impairments, conditions or disorders. Playfulness is vital in this 'hum-drum' world where children spend much of the day in wheelchairs or with specialised equipment, and routine is driven by personal/medical and care needs. Playful activities offer children a window of opportunity where they can become alive, fully engaged and interactive. On behalf of children with PMLD/SLD: 'more playfulness please!'

Time, all too often, as many of us know, proves to be the enemy. In this busy space, eating and drinking programmes and personal care are usually facilitated by a limited number of staff and this can lead to 'dead time' for children not actively involved. Problems, for me, arise when children are left sitting in 'arrivals and departures', waiting for something to happen, on and off throughout the day. This waiting 'space' is often filled thoughtfully and creatively by a single practitioner 'holding the fort'. Perhaps consider having pre-prepared bags or boxes, containing 'holding' creative interactive activities that can be delivered to a small group by a single practitioner.

Challenging behaviour/boundaries

Playful environments enable learners to find new and improved ways of doing things (Parker-Rees, 1999) but when children have challenging behaviour it may be necessary to control and regulate playfulness in order to keep arousal levels at an optimum level. Playfulness can improve the learning experience because it is motivating and engaging for a child who is functioning at a level similar to an infant.

There are many layers involved in children's challenging behaviour and the complex nature of some individuals can be overwhelming. I, like many of you, I suspect, struggle to manage ongoing issues with certain children. Reflecting upon behavioural issues with colleagues, discussing possibilities with others and seeking child-friendly solutions are important.

Considerations

- All behaviours have a purpose, message and possible underlying anxiety.
- Behaviour is an intention to communicate or a response to internal or external issues.
- Children may challenge environments by being too playful (setting limits is important).
- A lot of challenging behaviour is playful and this may be a signal that a child is not coping in some way.

- Behaviours reinforce the fact that there is an inability to communicate something that is important, or maybe it communicates that a child cannot communicate.
- Adults have differing views of children's playful behaviour and what is and is not acceptable.

To explore the issue of challenging behaviour, I spent time discussing playfulness and behaviour with teacher Val Stothard. I am grateful for her insightful contribution to this work. The following section presents the culmination of our thoughts. Our key judgement was that playfulness helps a child to learn about self-regulation and that, as adults, we assist them by demonstrating our ability to regulate our own behaviour.

Too much playfulness without authority (more like child-to-child play) results in a child not knowing when the adult is being serious; playfulness can escalate and the child may become over-excited and out of control; the child acts rudely and is then seen as behaving 'badly'. Many of us will be able to recall situations where playfulness between an adult and a child has become out of control. When this is the case, the adult may attempt to manage a child, who then becomes over-zealous and unruly by shouting, ignoring or using physical intervention in an attempt to regain control. In a final twist, a child may find the adult's extreme 'corrective' behaviour interesting or amusing, and this can escalate into a full-blown disagreement. A playful power struggle usually ends in 'tears'.

> If an adult allows too much playfulness without limits and boundaries, or before first establishing authority, the child will not regulate their own behaviour or understand that they need to. They will end up confused about adult expectations.

Practitioner voice

Adults must appear confusing at times for children because they hold different views and different levels of acceptance regarding playfulness. Much depends on an adults own life experience, their attitude to being playful and their confidence. The child unfortunately does not understand this when looking to the adult for guidance.

There is a balance, then, to be sought between playfulness and chaos caused by 'over-playfulness'. Consider this: if playfulness is used as a tool for developing self-regulation, over time the adult can withdraw control in the playful process so that the child learns to self-regulate their own behaviour, and this, in turn, helps them to keep themselves and others safe. Children are then independently able to guide and contribute to playful interaction with peers, as well as adults by their own behaviour and involvement. As time passes, the adult withdraws their control from a physical intervention to a word or a look. The child learns to read adult signals – what is acceptable and when and how to modulate their own behaviour – because this prolongs enjoyable and beneficial play times.

Using playfulness to manage behaviour

When a child is displaying arousal behaviours that could lead to challenging behaviour, the first step of intervention might be distraction and deflection using a light (playful) tone and manner. It is the opposite of being confrontational. When behaviour can be defused in this early stage it offers a child a way out. They do not lose face. The child is learning that they can have fun, that the adult enjoys being with them and that they are likeable. This provides a cornerstone to management because if the behaviour escalates, a stern, more serious, sombre style is needed. The contrast is marked and the effect noticeable. (Val Stothard)

In playfulness, as with many other aspects of education, adults need to take on a different role. However playful they are, they also need to provide an environment that is safe and respectful. Limits and boundaries need to be in place to protect a child emotionally as well as physically. This does not mean taking on an authoritarian stance, simply that boundaries are in place and the adult listens and actively responds to the child while also attending to their own behaviour. The child will learn about self-regulation through boundary and limit setting.

To illustrate:
Eric and four-year-old Michael were playing with two clothes pegs. Eric was hiding them on various parts of Michael's clothing. He was playful in his approach and used teasing to gain and maintain Michael's attention. Eric was challenging but didn't make things too difficult in order to guarantee Michael's success; he made use of surprise, playful facial expression and gasps to positively reinforce Michael's play behaviour. A turn-taking game ensued with Michael hiding pegs and trying to trick Eric. Both were having fun. Suddenly Michael attempted to put a peg on Eric's nose. Eric did not feel this was appropriate; he stopped using facial praise and pulled back for an instant to signal his discontent. Instead of using negative, dictatorial language and disapproval, Eric used distraction to re-engage Michael. Trickery, hiding the pegs and using questions like, 'How did that get there?', 'What's that doing on your collar?' or 'Who put that there?' ensured the interaction remained positive and the social learning continued.

What was Michael learning?

- that his ideas are valuable;
- that he is fun to be with;
- that he can make other people happy;
- to regulate his behaviour;
- how to use subtle body language and how body language conveys messages;
- the rules of turn-taking;
- alternative ways to behave;
- new ways of thinking and solving problems;
- developing an experimental frame of mind.

When children use playfulness to gain attention inappropriately – the class clown, for example – they need to be shown other ways to initiate play. This may be done through modelling or playful distraction. Ten-year-old Ginny, for example, often thrusts both arms forward to connect aggressively with an adult. Here, if the adult grasps Ginny's hands playfully, 'as if' the actions were a request to play, and proceeds to jiggle her arms and hands playfully, the aggressive element of the behaviour may be averted. In a similar way, John, when attempting to access out-of-bounds areas can be distracted by playing an anticipation or 'peek-a-boo' game. True, it's a juggling act, and there are few certainties, but in my experience, confrontation rarely serves to avert challenging behaviour.

Remember, too, that behaviours demand different techniques – some you can ignore and some you cannot. The issue of consistency is important because practitioners' moods can vary from day to day. A child can get mixed messages from a practitioner who sometimes ignores or tolerates behaviour while at other times reacts negatively. Different practitioners are likely to respond to behaviours differently. Thus, team support and discussion are vital to ensure consistency.

Adults with PMLD/SLD – the issue of age-appropriateness

I work mostly with school-age children and therefore the issue of age-appropriateness rarely enters my thoughts. I am, however, aware that, for others, especially those working in adult services, age-appropriateness may prove a barrier to playful experiences.

The principle of age-appropriateness refers to the use of activities and materials that are seen to be appropriate to a person's chronological age. While this may make a little sense, there is a real danger that obeying a 'rule' that does not actually exist as a developed concept (Hewett, 2011) results only in denying developmentally young adults enjoying a greater range of experiences: those that are most likely to be meaningful and appropriate considering their cognitive, social and emotional level.

I am currently working with a 21-year-old man with SLD and ASD. I find the principles of playful interaction to be virtually the same as those used with children but the essence of the interaction is somehow different. Adults are bigger and generally physically slower; they have a wealth of knowledge and experience from a life lived, and I am drawn to respect and dignify the interaction as an adult-to-adult dialogue.

During our time together:

- I will learn and use his language;
- I will take note of and value his developmental level and match his 'energy' so that our communication is appropriate and meaningful for him;
- I will endeavour to make the environment interesting, playful and engaging;
- I will not deny him an object or activity that might enrich his life, so long as there is no direct danger to him personally, to others or to property;
- I will offer him as many different objects and 'things' that I can think of to extend his experience of life;
- I want him to smile and gain a sense of satisfaction from his skill: I want to leave him with a sense of well-being;
- I want him to be able to celebrate who he is and not feel that he has to apologise for his different-ness or his special interests.

Playfulness is for everyone!

Postscript to Part I

By now I hope you have got the gist of my message. The playful space is sometimes kind yet often scary and harsh; it can be intimate or distant, quiet or loud, supportive but also challenging. It is a universe of fascination embracing the breadth and depth of social, emotional and cognitive reality. It is my firm belief that all of us would benefit from a little more playfulness not only in our practice but also in our life generally. I hope I have said and done enough to persuade you.

Part 2

Creative interactive activities

Chapter 7

Practitioner's starting point

Part 2 of this book offers a theoretical underpinning for new creative work linked to the use of Intensive interaction and the creative arts. Interactive music, interactive musical movement, finger dance, story and drama, artwork and reflective circle are presented, chapter by chapter, to underpin the interactive process and make clear the practical aspects of delivery.

For children with PMLD/SLD the potential space created by a framework of creative interactive activities is promising. The use of repetition of known and previously practised play routines breeds familiarity, predictability and security. When the atmosphere created is open and playful, there is likely to be an increase in interactivity; attention improves and new interests can emerge. There is something wonderfully fundamental and engaging about the use of music and the creative arts. It is my firm belief that creative interactive activities enable practitioners to facilitate cognitive, social and communication growth in helpful, engaging ways.

Playfulness is concerned with process since it is difficult to predict outcomes – you can't have prescriptive playfulness because of the richly spontaneous qualities inherent in the process. You do, however, in most cases, need to provide a safe, structured space, and the creative arts offer a perfect container for playful, interactive events.

Helping children to achieve their full intellectual potential is central in education but ensuring that they feel safe, valued and happy is arguably more important. The significance and value of facilitating a child's discovery through self-directed tasks should not be underestimated. Most parents, when asked about their hopes and aspirations for their children, simply stress that they want them to be happy. I am not suggesting that children with PMLD/SLD should be 'off' curriculum, rather that the curriculum and assessment process should reflect the reality of a child's world and that teaching is personalised to reflect a child's condition, strengths and difficulties. In education, offering a wide range of subjects in line with peers is important to ensure breadth and depth of experience for our PMLD/SLD learners.

The role of the facilitator in creative group work

The facilitator:

- plans the session and gathers together resources and props;
- ensures the space is safe;
- directs and guides the process;
- adopts an open, interactive style;
- empowers other practitioners to share leadership and lead activities;

- adds novelty, surprise and new activities to challenge and delight children;
- looks for windows of opportunity to engage and expand interactional dialogues;
- is highly responsive towards and can be controlled by the children – s/he is always attentive to individual's sounds and movements;
- is flexible enough to abandon structured activities in order to go with a particular child's flow;
- moves back and forth between group focus and individual focus;
- rewards children's efforts by using positive facial expressions and body language, affirming statements, smiles and laughter;
- initiates and shapes activities to ensure active learning;
- takes ultimate responsibility for recording outcomes or delegates this task to a fellow practitioner.

The role of fellow practitioners during group work

Practitioners:

- are helpful and show, through facial expression and body language, an exaggerated interest in the process;
- work with the facilitator to provide a highly interactive, enthusiastic, responsive environment;
- engage whole-heartedly in the process;
- engage and interact meaningfully with children;
- empower children to work independently;
- use prompts and cues thoughtfully and sensitively to enable children to access activities independently;
- use positive, reinforcing, affirming body language and facial expression when communicating with children;
- reward positive outcomes with smiles and affirming statements;
- keep children safe by attending sensitively to behavioural or personal care issues;
- share responsibility with the leader by taking a lead role from time to time;
- provide commentary if needed to alert the facilitator to any signals that may have been missed.

For all to consider

It is best to:

- set an example;
- show enjoyment, engagement and pleasure in the process;
- use exaggerated facial expression to show expectancy during game routines;
- use single words and simple phrases to communicate;
- use silent body language and facial expressions to manage behaviour;
- use subtle body language and facial expression to encourage participation;
- acknowledge achievement in ways appropriate to each individual;
- enable rather than help.

It is best to avoid:

- sitting back, with a glum look on your face, leaving all the 'work' and interaction to others;
- talking over the process about issues not related to the process;
- talking over children as if they weren't there;
- ignoring student achievement;
- taking over a child's active participation by helping too much;
- using hand-over-hand prompts until all other avenues of facilitation have been explored;
- enjoying the process so much that you forget you are there to engage and empower the child.

If we truly wish to engage with someone we need to learn and use their language. Play is the natural language of children, so perhaps it goes without saying that we need to be playful in order to make that all-important meaningful connection.

Group/individual

Many of the creative activities, games and songs presented in this book work equally well with individuals or small groups. They can be used on a one-to-one or one-to-two basis or incorporated into daily programmes if appropriate.

Tuning in to an individual during group work can be problematic and much depends on the team supporting the remaining individuals within the group. Good teamwork ensures group members are safe, reassured and thoughtfully engaged throughout the process.

Benefits of group work

Children can learn to:

- notice and interact with peers;
- become responsive to others' reactions;
- understand that actions have outcomes/consequences;
- communicate and make choices;
- read and notice signals and natural cues;
- listen, wait and take turns;
- practice developing skills;
- transfer skills learnt in one-to-one situations;
- enjoy and learn from another's performance;
- grow in confidence and improve self-esteem;
- celebrate together;
- self-regulate and co-operate.

Group work – questions and answers

Q. How long should sessions last?
A. Up to an hour but half to three-quarters is about right. A short 15-minute session can work well using favourite activities to gather, end or 'hold' a group.

Q. How many children in a group?

A. Six is perhaps ideal but much depends on ability levels and staffing. Group size can range from two to ten.

Q. How do you begin and end group work?

A. 'Something' should mark the beginning and end, and while activities may change according to topic themes, it helps when beginnings and endings stay roughly the same. Individual creative subject areas have their own identifying 'something' and this can be a point of reference for the child. A song, perhaps with a movement or a piece of music, can act as an opening activity. A particular instrument – Indian bells for example – may be used at the start of reflective circle time. Drums or music works for movement work and chants and rhymes for storytelling.

Q. Do sessions follow a particular pattern?

A. Some do. During interactive music I usually alternate between one whole-group activity – group parachute/lycra games, for example, and an individually focused game-song that requires a specific or spontaneous response. In all other sessions, when planning, I think about the flow and how sessions will serve to engage all the children. Always having a favourite game, object or song on stand-by serves to reconnect the group if things go awry. During interactive musical movement it works to have focused, quality one-to-one interactive episodes interspersed with time for self-directed, free-flow activities.

Figure 7.1 Tuning in

Chapter 8

Interactive music

Much of the early work and background concerning interactive music is documented in *Approaches to Communication through Music* (Corke, 2002). To reiterate: interactive music is an approach used in education and therapy; it stands alone in terms of motivating and gaining participation from some of our most difficult-to-reach children. Interactive music has a kind of enchantment because it is underpinned by sounds and music; it has an interactive quality that is playful and child-focused and the mood created through multisensory props and novel equipment holds the possibility of engaging and delighting children on many levels.

The process is child-centred and routines are developmentally appropriate to ensure children at all levels succeed. Interactive music, however, uses a behavioural frame (context) that is sufficiently firm to contain the uncertainties of a child-centred approach (process). The framework is behavioural in that there is a ritual, a routine and a perception of what is going to happen. The sequence of events and components, such as melodies and rewards, are known. Much of the behaviour is motivated by an anticipated outcome/reward – a horn sound, a tickle or splash of water, for example. The behavioural framework is important because it creates a 'safe' contained, predictable and secure space, which makes it easier for children to open up and participate. Flexibility within the process is paramount.

Most games and songs have an activity item (object of reference/visual cue) to help children anticipate what is going to happen next. This proves especially helpful for children with autism who are primarily visual learners. Familiar songs, known routines and structured activities offer reassurance and the facilitator presents instructions clearly and simply to further aid understanding. When new activities are introduced (it is important to offer changes regularly), great care has to be taken and the facilitator moderates input according to children's responses. During the process the facilitator takes on the role of attentive caregiver as s/he becomes 'stimulating, attentive, confirming, interpretive and highly supportive' (Trevarthen, cited in Hobson, 2002: 34).

When you discover a particular song or game that impacts at an emotional level – the ones that make a child smile or laugh – you know you have found a motivator and the key to the door of their inner world. This does not mean a particular game-song works for all; rather that children show preferences by the way they respond and, during interactive music, the adult reinforces their approval by repeating the activity and matching their engagement level. Once the 'feel-good factor' has been achieved, children are more likely to feel positive and secure in their response. Music and playful events help to capture children's attention and support social events.

The work of Prevezer (1991, 2000, 2002) is of particular importance because interactive music has its roots in Prevezer's work, but there are distinct differences. During musical interaction (validated by Wimpory and Nash, 1999), the therapist supports playful interactions between a child and an interactive partner using voice and a keyboard while paying 'detailed attention to timing, mood and energy' (Prevezer, 2000: 50). During interactive music, however, while supporting the group musically, the facilitator seeks to form relationships directly with each child and a range of multisensory props is incorporated throughout to enhance play routines.

Despite exploring many other creative tools over the past 25 years, I have not found any other approach that holds a small group of children with PMLD/SLD/ASD so well. If you haven't done so already – please give interactive music a go.

How does interactive music help?

Interactive music helps develop a child's knowledge, experience and imaginative understanding because of the creative and ever-changing content of sessions. Specific attributes and strengths are acknowledged and incorporated and this helps to develop a child's self-concept. The interactive nature of the approach ensures each child develops a form of communication that enables their needs to be communicated and encourages social communication to take place. Levels of playfulness help children to tolerate and enjoy social interaction with significant others and peers. Each child's strengths and interests are developed to the maximum and we help them to develop sufficient flexibility in order to cope with the demands of their social and physical environment. Importantly, too, there are opportunities for children to develop thinking and problem-solving skills to their maximum potential. Finally, interactive music helps learner's to express themselves, which nurtures a child's awareness of their own identity and that of others.

Helpful strategies to use during the process

- Think about the way you position instruments and props to facilitate independent, active exploration.
- Keep physical prompts to a minimum.
- When offering objects/instruments, wait and give time for your partner to reach or indicate a preference before proceeding.
- Give your partner enough time to ensure independent exploration.
- Celebrate every little achievement with gentle, affirming comments and positive body language.
- Enable your partner to play an instrument using their own style – a touch, scratch, rattle or push are just some of the possible exploration styles.
- Pause often in order to observe and reflect.
- Consider other access possibilities, for example holding an instrument near to a child's feet may empower them to elicit sounds.
- Try using a verbal/sung commentary.
- Of course, be playful and make it fun.

Problem-solving

- If instruments/objects are thrown, try seeing this action as initiating play: pick the item up and gently throw it back to create a two-way play routine. Do this for several repeats to establish a game and perhaps use your voice to complement the action – 'whee!' and so on.

- If items are pushed away you might like to turn this into a game. Try, for example, playfully over-exaggerating your response by saying pu...sh. A push away, however, may communicate 'no', so take a measured stance and respect a child's decision.
- Where movements are very slight, slow the pace right down, draw the instrument near to your partner and hold it still to allow the tiniest movement to be felt.
- When physical disability is marked, it might be important to hold the instrument quite still to enable a child to gain a sense of the item. Movements may be slight; prompts are rarely required but practitioner patience is vital. It will also be important to think about an individual's skill so that objects are offered in positions that best suit their individual physical ability.
- Most children with PMLD are learning to experiment and explore, not to 'play' an instrument, thus independent exploration through mouthing, touching, fiddling and looking are all-important developmental discovery stages.
- Try to establish joint attention. If a child looks at an object, look at it with them and draw attention to the fact by pointing and positively reinforcing their actions by your acknowledgement and measured movements/body language/commentary.

The following pages of this chapter present a range of tried-and-tested interactive music game-songs, including music score. Interactive music game-songs have been devised to extend interaction and develop fundamental communication and sociability (Corke, 2002). It helps to read music, and children love the guitar, but the tunes are very simple and no particular musical skill is required, just a willingness to have a go. If 'worst comes to worst', use the game-songs by simply chanting/saying the words or try using well-known tunes with the game-song words.

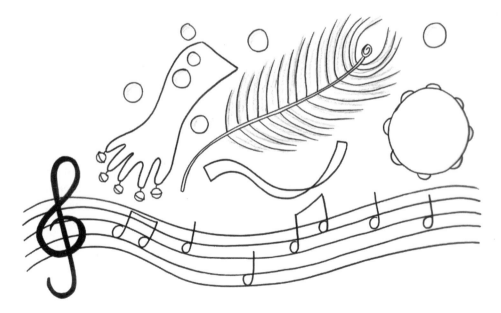

Figure 8.1 Musical adventures

Be a Clown for Today

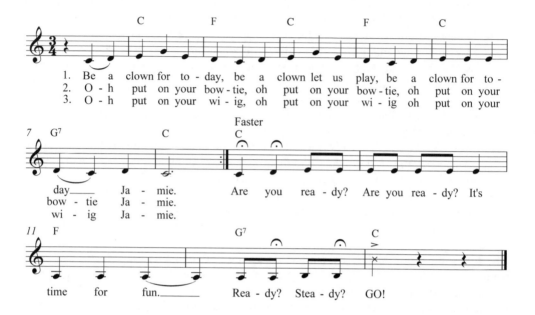

Figure 8.2 Be a Clown for Today

Resources: Clown wig, large bow tie and duck call whistle. I keep all these together in a small cloth bag.

Game-song: The facilitator dresses up within the structure of the song. Go at a steady pace and repeat the song during the process if necessary. Take every opportunity to interact with the children; be playful, have fun! When you reach the phrase 'Are you ready for fun', say 'Ready steady', pause expectantly, wait for a signal from a particular individual, then deliver the playful sounds of a duck call whistle or similar. The playful clown may lean forwards and engage individual students during the dressing-up process. A child may show particular interest in your wig, and this, once again, helps to draw attention to your face. Enjoy being playful.

Extension ideas/activities

- If a student wants to feel, explore or wear the wig/outfit, enable this and go with the flow of their ideas for a while. Perhaps they want to try it on.
- A duck call whistle, as well as offering a quick, sharp sound, is particularly good for creating non-verbal conversational sounds.

- Try using a duck call whistle to mirror a child's movement with sound.
- Try imitating a student's laughter with tones from the duck call whistle – great fun!
- Instead of 'ready steady go', you could use 'one, two, three' (an instant maths game).
- Enable children to dress up and take a lead role when the child is able to understand the process. Children's attempts may require patience and a few subtle prompts to ensure their success.

Can You Feel the Beat?

Figure 8.3 Can You Feel the Beat?

Resources: Wooden claves or similar.

Game-song: The facilitator moves around the inner circle, singing the song while tapping the claves together in time with the rhythm. A child's name is chosen and the facilitator moves towards that student and then rhythmically taps out their particular name.

Extension ideas/activities

- Gently imitate the beat on a child's body in time with the claves.
- Use a drum or other percussion instrument instead of claves.
- Use a pattern of words that link to a particular topic or seasonal theme.
- Another version of this can be useful as a greeting activity – this concerns rhythmically beating the child's name and surname, three times, adding 'here today' at the end.

Feel What You're Feeling

Figure 8.4 Feel What You're Feeling

Resources: Saris, sarongs, silk scarves etc. or sensory stimuli to suit your need.

Game-song: This is a song about the senses. The song may generate a feeling of relaxation and calm.

Extension ideas/activities

- Consider using survival blankets, water sprays, perfume sprays etc.
- Use this song with a sensory box containing items to feel and explore.
- This song can be used in a variety of settings to encourage relaxation.
- This a repetitive tune. Perhaps try singing the words a few times and then hum the tune several times before going back to words again as this can aid relaxation.

Relaxation

Relaxation concerns being free from tension and anxiety – a state that can be triggered by an appropriate environment, nature, music, sound, touch or nurturing physical contact.

I'm Huffing and Puffing

Figure 8.5 I'm Huffing and Puffing

Resources: A balloon pump. Plastic rectangular tube types are my favourite. These are relatively easy to decorate with, for example, holographic tape. Decorating a 'pump' helps to make it more distinctive and special.

Game-song: Move around the inner circle huffing and puffing the balloon pump. This creates a nice 'huffing' sound to gain children's attention. With a particular child in mind, move towards them and pause expectantly. After the final sung phrase, 'huffing and puffing', wait for a child to signal then deliver three puffs of wind as you say: 'atchoo, atchoo, atchoo'. Sensitivity towards students' wishes is paramount when delivering the puffs of wind. Ask yourself, 'Are they okay with this', 'Should I puff on their hands or a foot instead of their face'. (Be aware that a puff to the face may feel threatening.)

Extension ideas/activities

- A child may say 'atchoo' to signal a desire for a puff of wind.
- At Christmas time I use a balloon pump when singing 'When Santa Got Stuck Up the Chimney' and add a burst–pause moment when Santa sneezes at the end.

Fifth of November

Please re-mem-ber the fifth of No-vem-ber, it's Bon-fire Night, it's Bon-fire Night.

Please re-mem-ber the fifth of No-vem-ber. Wizz bang spar-kle it's Bon-fire Night.

Figure 8.6 Fifth of November

Resources: Pompoms, ribbon sticks (made by attaching ribbons or strong holographic gift wrap to a balloon stick or similar), party poppers (if appropriate) etc.

Game-song: This is a simple song to support a seasonal theme. Sensitivity towards students' wishes is paramount as ever. N.B. Take care with sudden or loud sounds, especially with blind and visually impaired children. Unexpected sounds delivered without pre-warning may startle, and while this may serve to arouse, it may cause fear and anxiety. Children who are blind have no visual cueing system and benefit from the use of a verbal/touch cue to inform them of an impending loud sound.

Extension ideas/activities

- A parachute can be used. Each time you sing, 'Its bonfire night', lift the parachute. Linger when the parachute is up so that the children can enjoy the view. Useful as a group burst–pause activity.

Interactive Shakers

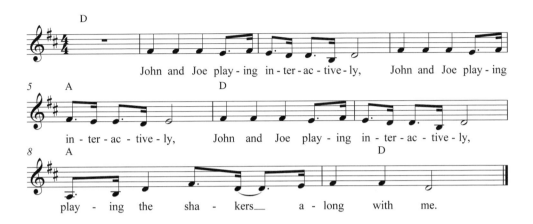

Figure 8.7 Interactive Shakers

Resources: Two 'high juice' squash bottles (the ones that have a neck because this feels like a handle – easy to hold and manipulate). You can use other objects in the same way but the shakers are effective because you can squeeze, shake, bang and watch the visual effects inside the bottle. Fill each bottle identically. Ideas for filling include beads, tiny plastic spiders, foil confetti, anything sparkly and so on. Seal the lid with strong tape (holographic tape works well if you can source it).

Game-song: The song accompanies the interaction – two people, usually one adult and one child holding a shaker. The adult usually sits themselves in front of the child, available, observing and ready to copy the child's moves (intensive interaction with a prop). There are developmental stages to this interactive game.

Step by step

1. Practitioner copies child – child is unaware of their partner's shaker.
2. Practitioner copies child – child glances tentatively and becomes aware of their partner's shaker (aware that there is more than one).
3. Practitioner copies child – child becomes aware that the adult is copying them and shows this by glancing with interest.
4. Practitioner copies child but makes one highly defined move (like patting the shaker gently on their own head or foot) and waits to see if the child imitates. If a child does not imitate, the practitioner goes back to imitating the child.
5. Practitioner copies the child but makes one highly defined move. The child imitates that particular move and the practitioner tentatively offers another move (tap on head then hand, for example). N.B. In the first instance subtle moves do not work.

6. Practitioner and child can imitate each other and take turns leading
7. Two children play the interactive shaker game. They have to negotiate turns and think of ever-increasing moves to challenge the other.

Extension ideas/activities

*   I add to my repertoire of shakers all the time, making new ones to support seasonal or topic themes.
*   With more able children, another idea involves everyone holding a shaker – one person leads and others copy.
*   Endless opportunities for musical skill development (fast-slow, loud-quiet etc., and copying patterns and rhythms etc.
*   When using this game-song during group work, and more than one couple have a set of shakers, it helps to change the words to: 'play with the shakers interactively'.
*   Having additional shakers in your bag may be helpful for children with a heightened interest so that they can go on exploring while the game continues with other children.

Lycra Pull Game

Resources: Length of four-way-stretch lycra – size two to three metres depending on group size.

Game–chant: The chant accompanies the game. When I reach the 'tighter, tighter' phrase I build tension by slowing and pulling the lycra, and by using rising intonation to increase tension further until you let go.

'Pull, pull, pull it out. Shake it, shake it all about. Pull, pull, pull it out,
Tighter, tighter, tighter..........Let go!'

Extension ideas/activities

*   Place a suitable cuddly toy on the lycra. Chant 'one, two, three' and make the toy go high. Alternatively, shake the lycra up and down until the toy falls off and then use this opportunity to ask questions concerning prepositions. Say, for example, 'Where's the big bird' as you place it on/under the lycra or under your arm, on your head etc.
*   Use any song that has a repeated word/phrase – the lycra is lifted each time the word/phrase is sung. For example, 'God Save Our Gracious Queen'. Simply, each time you sing 'queen', the lycra is lifted. Take the game at a steady pace and enjoy the view underneath.

Look into the Bag

Figure 8.8 Look into the Bag

Resources: A colourful cloth bag that is big enough for you to be able to hold on to it in a closed position. Objects of your choice to go inside.

Game-song: Sing the song while holding and rattling the bag to gain attention and a sense of anticipation. Either sit with the bag in front of you or move around the inner circle teasingly. Offer an open bag to an individual and the rest is up to you. What's inside may be topic-linked, seasonal or simply something interesting or funny. If a child can name or describe the object go with this, if not, an adult can name and describe using very simple language.

Step by step

1. A child is offered an object, taken from the bag, to explore. Encourage a reach-for gesture.
2. A child puts their hand in the bag and takes out an object to freely explore.
3. Use verbal cue 'take one'.
4. A child is encouraged to relinquish the object into the bag when their turn has finished. It helps to use the phrase 'in the bag' as a verbal prompt.
5. A child makes a choice from more than one object in the bag and explores freely.
6. A child makes a choice from more than one object in the bag and the adult provides a spoken commentary about their moves.
7. A child is asked to make a particular choice from more than one object in the bag.
8. A child makes a choice from more than one object in the bag by naming the object to request access.
9. A child makes a choice from more than one object in the bag and describes colour, shape, properties etc.

Extension ideas/activities

- Ring the changes and add surprises (novel, unexpected or funny items).
- If this game is to be successful the objects inside need to reflect the children's special/high interests. Instruments can work well.
- Create a set of matching symbols or photographs to use within a picture trading system, e.g. PECS (Bondy and Frost, 1994).
- When using this game-song it is helpful to change the words from 'describe' to 'feel' as appropriate.

River

Figure 8.9 River

Resources: A blue piece of material, parachute or lycra.

Game-song: This is a gentle song to support a water theme. Use a piece of material to waft and create a watery scene.

Extension ideas/activities

- Blue pompoms or ribbons can work well with this song and these can be used interactively.
- Consider using water-sounding instruments: rain-maker, ocean drum etc.
- This song can be used to accompany rocking back and forth, perhaps to aid relaxation.

Marvellous Magician

Figure 8.10 Marvellous Magician

Resources: A wizard hat and a magician-type hat for hiding chosen objects, and a 'magic' cloth to cover and hide objects placed in the hat. Objects to hide might include a small car, a fish, a ball, a spoon etc.

Game-song: Start by preparing to hide two objects. Show the objects to the group. The song then begins and the wizard, a chosen practitioner who wears the wizard's hat, moves around the inner circle. He/she holds an empty hat and puts the objects inside, making sure children view the objects in the hat. The hat is then covered with the magic cloth and the chosen object is secretly removed while the song is sung. The magic cloth is used to disguise the withdrawal. Walk towards a student as the magic cloth is whisked off to reveal a missing object. The question is posed, 'What's missing in here?' and a pause is created to enable the student to formulate a response. The cloth re-covers the hat and the missing object is secretly placed back inside. Use magic words like 'Abracadabra' to reveal the reappeared object. Outcomes will vary depending on ability.

Extension ideas

- Begin by hiding just one object. For more able groups, the number of objects can be increased.
- A single object can be used when attempting to develop object permanence.
- When appropriate, a child can take a lead role. Gentle prompts can be used to ensure success.
- The wizard's hat can be used for 'hat on/hat off' games.

Wet, Wet, Wet

(words to the tune of 'Quarter Master's Store')

'It is wet, wet, very, very, wet in the rain, in the rain.
It is wet, wet, very, very, wet in the pouring, pouring rain'.

Resources: Water–spray pot.

Game–song: As you sing, squirt a spray of water in the air to set the scene. Approach a child on the second round of the song and pause before the word 'wet' ('It is ...'). When the child signals or says 'wet', offer a water squirt (there are two opportunities for a 'wet' pause in this song. When using water sprays try to find one that shoots a mist of water instead of a jet. Spray up and around before a child is 'targeted'; this creates a landscape of wetness rather than a downpour! Great care is needed so as not to frighten or threaten children with water and the face is rarely the place to start when squirting. Try hands and feet first and, of course, read body language signals and facial expressions to guide your actions and responses.

Extension ideas/activities

- When children find the water spray threatening, perhaps practitioners might be up for a squirt instead!
- Change 'rain' to 'sea' and 'the pouring, pouring rain' to 'blue and briny sea', for a seaside theme.

Saris of India

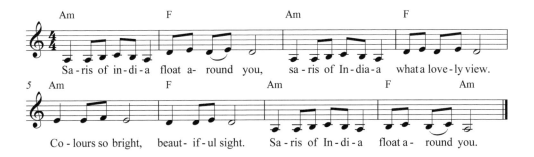

Figure 8.11 Saris of India

Resources: Sari material length(s).

Game-song: The more saris you have the better, but if you only have one, that's fine too. Two adults hold the sari over the children and waft it up and down. Wafting happens best when both sari ends go up together. The arms then stay up until the sari begins to float downwards, and then repeat.

Extension idea/activity

- On occasions when you might have enough staff to use several saris at once, you can create what is known as a 'sari star' (thank you to an excellent trainer, Barbara, for this idea, some 15 years ago when I attended special music workshops at Trinity College of Music in London). Try eight adults and four saris. Layer one sari over the other like a star. Each set of adults lift their sari up, one at a time, top one first. The next follows, then the next, and when all four are up you have created a lovely sari star.
- With just one adult you simply play with the sari: shake it up and down, lay it on children's laps, wrap it around their body, hide underneath it etc.
- Sari's can be held at the top of one end to form a wall-like drape. Hold it still so that children can enjoy the visual qualities of the material and pattern. This gives time, too, for children to reach out and touch in their own time.
- Sari's can be held by two adults, each holding one corner and this is then draped back and forth from one side of a room to the other over children who may be lying on the floor.

Sunshine Parachute

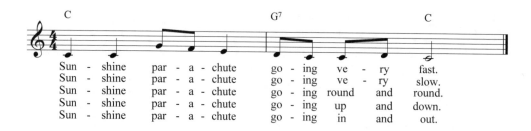

Sun - shine	par - a - chute	go - ing	ve - ry	fast.
Sun - shine	par - a - chute	go - ing	ve - ry	slow.
Sun - shine	par - a - chute	go - ing	round and	round.
Sun - shine	par - a - chute	go - ing	up and	down.
Sun - shine	par - a - chute	go - ing	in and	out.

Figure 8.12 Sunshine Parachute

Resources: A group-size parachute – yellow and orange is ideal but use whatever you have. SeamStress offer a wonderful range of parachutes to suit all group sizes (info@playchutes.com).

Game-song: Song accompanies the game. Sing 'Sunshine Parachute', pause after 'going' and wait for a child to signal. In group work, watch especially carefully during the pause to pick up on the smallest attempt to signal. I often use simply up and down/fast and slow phrases in turn when first introducing the song.

Extension ideas/activities

- Sing 'rainbow' (multi-coloured), 'spooky' (black and navy) or 'snowy' (white) parachute or link with different parachutes/topic.
- Children love to go under. We can go with their flow and this is fun, but take care: it's a balancing act between playfulness and chaos!
- With more able groups, swapping places when names are called is very popular.
- Use the 'Wheels on the Bus' tune and sing: 'The blue parachute goes up and down' for similar effect. Pause after 'goes'.

Whistles and Blowers

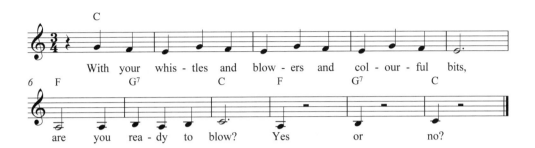

Figure 8.13 Whistles and Blowers

Resources: Whistles/party blowers or sound makers.

Game-song: You can wear a fun, colourful costume for this one. Have a bag of wind instruments ('blowers'), or one or two, or simply a favourite party blower. Move around the inner circle, interacting and teasing the children. After singing: 'are you ready to blow', pause and wait for a response. Once a child signals, you can blow the whistle, perhaps tentatively, perhaps playfully, to cause lots of smiles and laughter.

Extension ideas/activities

- It's fun to have a bag full of lots of different whistles, wind instruments, sound makers and 'blowers'.
- Simple plastic party horns are popular.
- It is best to have some antibacterial wipes to hand.
- The 'yes or no' ending to this song is optional, dependent on ability.

The Floating Scarves

The___ floa - ty scarves go up and down, up and down and all a - round and it's go - ing o - ver Ja - mie.

Figure 8.14 The Floating Scarves

Resources: Silky scarves or similar.

Game-song: Waft the scarf/scarves up and down and all around in line with the words of the song. Move towards an individual, and as you sing 'and it's going over', pause for a signal. Put a scarf over the child's head. Hopefully, the child will take the scarf off and a 'boo' moment can then occur. When using scarves to cover children's faces, ensure that they are the 'see-through' type: it can be frightening for some children to suddenly be thrown into darkness.

Extension ideas/activities

- It can be useful to playfully hide practitioners in the process as this may help children learn about object permanence, and it's fun.
- This works well with individuals or groups.
- Sing 'Where is …' to extend the hiding game.

Interactive Game

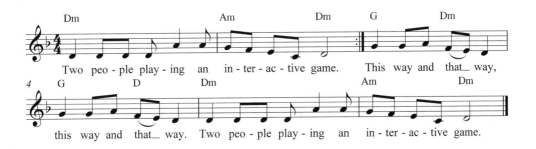

Figure 8.15 Interactive Game

Resources: Pairs of objects – perhaps slinky, silky scarves, scrunches, squidgy toys, instruments etc.

Game-song: This is song to support joint attention. Each pair has the same objects. The child takes the lead and the practitioner follows and interacts accordingly. Similarly, a single object can be used as the centre of attention and here the practitioner tentatively shares the object with the child. The practitioner enables the child to lead and offers a sensitive spoken or sung commentary if and when appropriate.

Extension ideas/activities

- A child's favourite activity item can be used – elastic bands, Blu-Tack and 'twiddle' bits, for example.

Interaction is Our Way

Figure 8.16 Interaction is Our Way

Resources: Pairs of objects/hiding cloths.

Game-song: This song supports interaction with or without objects and can be used as a kind of 'peek-a-boo' game – playfully hiding and finding each other. There are lots of opportunities for joint attention.

Extension ideas/activities

- If using a hiding cloth, you can change the final phrase within the song to 'play peek-a-boo'.
- A nice extension to this activity is: after a verse is sung a round of humming or vocal play 'do do do-be-do' (same tune) can be sung before returning again to verse. Without words, the 'do-be-do' bit can be carried on for as long as necessary.

Quietly, Go to Sleep

Figure 8.17 Quietly, Go to Sleep

Resources: Not required, although you could use small blankets.

Game-song: Children are encouraged to close their eyes or rest quietly. A short period of quiet is created before the wake-up part of the song. The wake-up arrives suddenly and is fast and furious, which usually causes great delight once the routine is learnt. Repeat this song several times for the best effect.

Extension ideas/activities

- The final two phrases in this song can change to reflect what children do – 'stamp your feet' and so on, instead of 'yawn and stretch'.

Playing Quiet Sounds

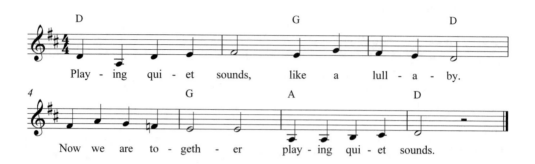

Figure 8.18 Playing Quiet Sounds

Resources: Instruments that create quiet sounds.

Game-song: This is song to support gentle instrumental work or it can be used during relaxation with a single instrument playing quietly in the background.

Extension ideas/activities

- You can add a second verse – 'Playing loud sounds like a thunder storm', etc.
- You might consider offering a range of instruments, loud and quiet, and change what you sing to match children's playing (improvising). To explain further: the above song is sung quietly but when anyone makes louder sounds this acts as a trigger to change tempo and dynamic as you slip into verse two for a while before returning to the quieter verse one. Use for many repeats.

Boom, Boom, Boom

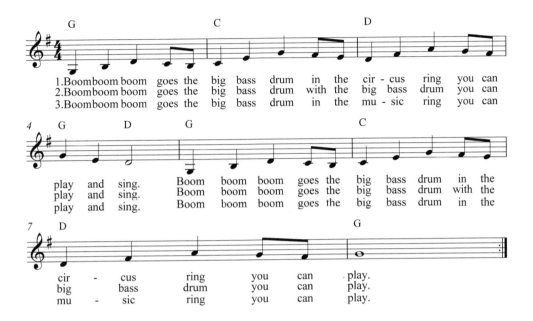

Figure 8.19 Boom, Boom, Boom

Resources: A big drum (bodhrun or buffalo drum work best).

Game-song: Move around the inner circle playing the drum. A child can elicit sounds/play whenever you direct the drum towards them. While exploring a drum, a child may like to turn it over; play with the strings (buffalo drum), tap the side, lick/mouth the drum etc. Remember, children are at the experimenting/exploring stage if they do not elicit a sound independently or show a desire to play a pattern.

Extension ideas/activities

* This song works well linked to a circus theme.
* When using this song in a one-to-one situation, turn-taking games can ensue. Here the song is used like a chorus with the drumming happening like a verse.
* Some children might be able to take a lead role and take centre stage. They can choose and approach a peer/adult and enable them to elicit sounds from the drum.

Boom-whackers

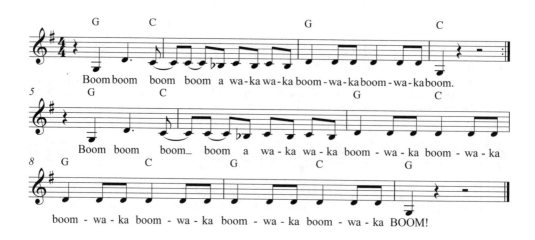

Figure 8.20 Boom-whackers

Resources: Boom-whackers.

Game-song: Simple song to support sound-making and exploration using boom-whackers.

Extension ideas/activities

- It is good if the practitioner can create sound patterns on boom-whackers while children are freely exploring and experimenting with the qualities of these cylindrical tuned tubes.
- Boom-whackers can be used to play 'peek-a-boo'.
- Boom-whackers can be used for vocal sound-making and vocal play.

Changes in the Weather

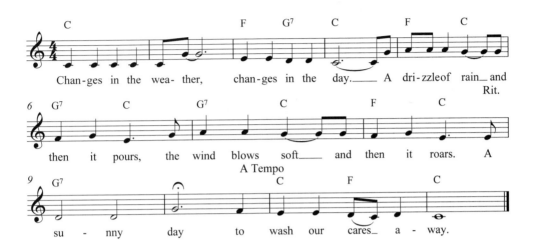

Figure 8.21 Changes in the Weather

Resources: Water, a fan and small yellow wafting cloth.

Game-song: Use resources to accompany song in line with the words. Sing the song through once; then sing again slowly to allow time for presentation of props. Each section can be repeated as necessary.

Extension ideas/activities

• You can use this song to accompany a massage.

Link action to word:

    changes – jiggle one side of the body then the other;
    drizzle – tapping fingers on back;
    pours – fingers running downwards on back;
    wind – hands side-to-side on back;
    roars – rubbing hands faster side-to-side;
    sunny day – draw big circle using hand on back;
    wash – both hands on head and gently falling down either side of the body.

Bells

Figure 8.22 Bells

Resources: Bells.

Game-song: A simple tune to support play and exploration/experimentation using bells.

Extension ideas/activities

- When using bells or any other instruments, try to have a variety of types to encourage exploration on many levels, choice-making, colour recognition, size and so on.
- At Christmas-time, children love 'Jingle Bells'. Sing the chorus but instead of singing 'dashing through the snow', try using individual names as a sung commentary: 'John plays the bells, John plays the bells, John plays the bells, oh, John plays the bells', then sing 'Jingle Bells' again, and so on.

May Day

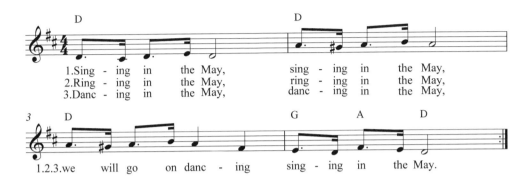

Figure 8.23 May Day

Resources: Ribbon sticks and bells. Ribbon sticks can be colourful – florist ribbon works well as it can be shred into different widths and it's very strong. Crêpe paper also works surprisingly well. Plastic balloon sticks are good and it's easy to attach ribbons by tying on to the plastic head.

Game-song: A simple song to enhance a May Day theme.

Extension ideas/activities

- It is good to have lots of movement and dancing whenever possible. Change places, have individual performances or mirror your partner in turn-taking exchanges.

Chapter 9

Interactive musical movement

The development of interactive musical movement (IMM) has concerned moulding, shaping and recreating ideas over time to form a simplistic, interactive dance approach for people with PMLD/SLD that can be facilitated by specialist and non-specialist alike.

Why movement and dance?

A 'dance' space offers physical freedom and increased opportunities for interaction on many levels – perfect! Moving and playing interactively gives children opportunities to learn through body sensations, feelings and through cycles of visual, physical and tactile feedback. In this space, carefully chosen music and sensory props:

- help to create a mood;
- provide opportunities for play and exploration;
- enhance and extend thematic/topic work;
- foster relationships (props are used as a bridge to communication);
- encourage children to move in different ways;
- encourage creative responses;
- help to raise cultural awareness;
- help develop responsiveness to music through movement;
- promote choice-making;
- increase interactive possibilities.

IMM is concerned with fostering relationships; it is about practitioners being open to movement possibilities and tuning in physically and emotionally. Going with the flow of a child's movements, while also maintaining a physical presence, creates opportunities for intensive interaction and joint action/attention routines. 'Synchrony, sharing of body rhythms and playful mirroring of actions, establishes that basic feeling of being-at-one-with-the-other, and of being effortlessly understood' (Naess, 1982: 46).

While IMM is not directly a dance and movement approach (there is no specific desire to teach dance, improve motor skills or offer therapy), it has evolved, to some extent, from the work of dance and movement specialists. Occupational therapists, physiotherapists, storytellers, performing artists and inspired special needs practitioners have, over time, also influenced my thinking in the development of this interactive approach.

Principle influences

Veronica Sherborne

Sherborne's contribution to special education is important. She began to develop ideas about ways of working with children in the mid-1950s. Her work was greatly influenced by Laban (1948) whose analysis of movement has provided practitioners with a framework for analysis and assessment of movement. Inspired by Laban's work, Sherborne began to explore ways of reaching children with special needs. Her belief was that children 'need to feel at home in their own bodies . . . and they need to be able to form relationships' (Sherborne 2001: xiii).

Laban coined the phrase 'free dance' to explain the dancer's free expression of feelings and inner self. Essentially, movement was seen as awareness of space; development of an individualised movement vocabulary and creativity. Sherborne explored these ideas focusing, in particular, on self-expression and creativity so as to improve relationships and develop movement confidence of children. Her work was driven by a desire to be completely sensitive towards learners and to encourage partners to develop mutual trust as part of an expressive process.

Jabadeo

Many years ago I purchased an inspiring handbook on creative dance work with children (Crichton and Greenland, 1994). It offered an abundance of activities and strategies to encourage children to 'notice their own dances'. This, the authors explained, could help children learn through mindful, self-directed play (p. 2). The main thrust of the Jabadeo approach was to work non-judgementally; to help children 'release the movement that is naturally theirs and to play with it' (p. 2). This notion, coupled with the underpinning philosophy of intensive interaction, seems to describe what I try to achieve in IMM.

Practitioner role

Partners playing co-actively with movement ideas discover movement repertoires within the free flow of dance. The practitioner role is one of encouraging and extending interactive ability by being available, non-judgemental, playful and utterly responsive. Movement patterns expressed by individuals are often instinctive – we each seem to have our own internal rhythm to play with and extend. Importantly, Ayres (1979) reminds us that an individual's drive to move in particular ways is driven, in part, by biological factors. Children become increasingly open to learning when their subjective experience is acknowledged and valued – children are the choreographers in this dance event: follow their lead!

Figure 9.1   Interactive dance

Golden rules

- Use intensive interaction; actively observe and respond to the child's interests and movement pattern and alter what you are doing to exaggerate and extend the child's expressive moves.
- Strive to create opportunities for joint-attention and joint-action routines. Props are helpful in this regard.
- Use playfulness to engage children in games and playful routines.
- Consider taking a lead role; use a particular movement or movement pattern previously undertaken by a child (something they already have in their repertoire) to interest them. Go back to following the child if they show no interest.
- Experiment with movement in the context of your props. Try simple actions in and around a student to encourage tracking and physical/visual responses. Again watch for a reaction; do not dominate the interaction – joining them and using their ideas generally works best.
- See if a child will imitate your moves (mirroring activities). When a child can imitate your actions, the interaction moves on to a new level where turn-taking activities and simple dance routines can be 'played' with.
- Value the child's ideas, which are likely to be very different to your own.
- Take time and go at the pace of the child – sometimes very slowly, acknowledging tiny finger movements or head moves when movement repertoire is limited.
- Be genuine and enjoy!

Intensive interaction is at the heart of this approach but it might be helpful to explore and adapt approaches such as contact improvisation to further extend opportunities for physical contact awareness.

Contact improvisation

Contact improvisation is a dance form in which the point of contact with another dancer provides the starting point for a movement exploration. It is about sharing weight, rolling, suspending, falling, passive and active, energy and awareness (Contact Improvisation UK, accessed online 2/1/11).

Key features

Space

A large room is best; most likely the school hall. Remove as many distractions as possible. Place mats on the floor to one side. Sometimes children will lie or sit throughout a session where it might feel most comfortable for them. IMM happens where the child is – there is no compulsion for them to go to the 'dance' space, rather the dance space exists wherever they are. Practitioners support the child by staying in close proximity; they are open to the child's interactive moves, which may be subtle, slight or active. It may be desirable for a child to remain in their wheelchair (wheelchair dancing can be invigorating and fun) but a child, most likely, will enjoy the freedom and movement possibilities offered by the floor or a mat. Go with the movement flow created by individual children.

Structure

Crichton and Greenland (1994) wisely suggest that while freedom of movement is paramount, there needs also to be firm, strong 'holding' to avoid chaos. They recommend a good balance between boundaries and space and I whole-heartedly agree. Thus themes and activities are delivered within a structured framework: a session plan incorporating a list of interactive dance activities. The process, however, remains largely flexible: intensive interaction techniques are used to connect with children and props enhance the space and encourage movement. Playfulness helps to engage children in joint-action routines and the music sets the scene and mood for each dance.

Music

Music provides a backdrop for the 'dance' and can be used to support a theme or topic. Music is especially helpful because it can trigger emotional responses leading to movement and dance-like behaviours.

During the planning stage, when making music choices, listen to the rhythm. Close your eyes and try to visualise the 'scene' and how to incorporate and use props. The music can act as a reference point for the child especially when certain props are regularly linked with a particular piece of music.

Drums and percussion instruments can enhance the dance space but take care that they do not dominate or overpower; better that they add a dynamic interlude at beginning middle or end.

Props

Props act as 'movement motivators': ribbons (on sticks and in different lengths, colours etc.); hoops, saris, sarongs, lycra lengths, all kinds of material to support different themes; parachutes, feathers, fans, masks, umbrellas, silk scarves, gloves, survival blankets, plastic whirly, pompoms and so on: these are just some of the props that work well in a dance space. Use your imagination – think outside the box.

IMM concerns interaction; thus it is helpful to provide each practitioner and child with the same prop at each stage of the 'dance story'. Practitioners join the child – they imitate, experiment, play and reinforce movement and interaction ideas.

N.B. Please ensure all equipment used is safe and child-friendly. I find it helpful to keep equipment in a bag or box and use one set of props at a time.

Movement possibilities to play with

Some movements may originate from inner sensations and body rhythms, some can appear 'odd' and others disorganised, but when accompanied by music a child's moves create a real sense of dance. With PMLD children you will also be considering facial expression, lip, finger movements and muscle movements. Reflex actions as well as intentional moves, natural gestures and stillness can all form part of the often intimate dance routine.

Children may present as passive or active (sometimes overactive!); there may be big, strong movements or tentative, fragmented ones. Remember also that eye contact, glancing, head turning and facial expressions all form part of a unique and special dance. More gross motor movements will include turning, twisting, rising and sinking, bending and stretching, parting and meeting; jumping, swaying and rocking. Let them surprise you, and yes, it can be physically tiring!

Shaping a session

Firstly, consider setting boundaries: 'We stay in the room, no climbing on chairs, no unhelpful behaviour towards others, keep safe'. Make sure fellow practitioners know the 'rules'.

As with most approaches, it works well to have a gathering/introductory activity. For some groups this may involve a physical warm-up to music; further options include using a song, drumming, chants or body drama (sensitive patting on the body, in time with a particular piece of music). Endings (the cool down) usually involve relaxation, a farewell song or gentle rocking to music.

It is important, when planning, to think about the shape of a session. A theme can run for several weeks creating a sense of familiarity and increase movement repertoire/interactive outcomes. I have tried various models when using IMM and much depends on the ability level of children and the dynamics of the group.

Model 1: Gathering and greeting. Think beginning – middle (dance activities) – end.

Model 2: Gathering and greeting and 'chorus' (a chorus is an activity, chant or song repeated between each dance). For example: gathering, thematic dance/event – 'chorus' – thematic dance/event – 'chorus' – relaxation – farewell. (See sample session plan on the following page.)

Model 3: Gathering and greeting. Free-flow improvisation – a single theme is introduced through music without the use of props or with limited props. A simplified form of contact improvisation works well here with all group members involved (contact improvisation in this context means simply waiting for a child to initiate contact, then moving with them while maintaining physical contact during the interactive process if possible) or with one-to-one in the same way.

I have included a sample session plan using Model 2 to demonstrate the process.

INTERACTIVE MUSICAL MOVEMENT		
Topic theme: Environment		
Inspiration: *Oi! Get Off Our Train*, John Burningham (1991)		
ACTIVITY	INTERACTIVE DANCE	MUSIC TYPE
Greeting	Chant: 'High, low say hello'. Greet and dance, tap hand high and low and sign hello	Line dance
All aboard *Train*	Row of chairs like a train placed at side of hall	Train sounds
Stomping/marching *Elephant*	Interaction using plastic whirlies (because they are like an elephant trunk)	Walt Disney's *Jungle Book*: 'Colonel Hathi Elephant March'
All aboard *Train*	Row of chairs like a train at side of hall	Train sounds
Benches and balance boards or/and big and small balls/hoops *Seal*	Bouncing on large physiotherapy balls, throwing, rolling or catching balls and hoops Balancing on benches	Circus
All aboard *Train*	Row of chairs like a train at side of hall	Train sounds
Body awareness Blowing *Crane*	Interactive tickling games using feathers	*Swan Lake*
All aboard *Train*	Row of chairs like a train at side of hall	Train sounds
Hide and chase *Tiger*	Someone hides under a large piece of faux tiger fur – practitioners say the chant and a 'coming to get you' game ensues	Chant: Tiger, tiger where are you? In the jungle or in the zoo. Tiger, tiger looking for your tea. Tiger, tiger come and get me.
All aboard *Train*	Row of chairs like a train at side of hall	Train sounds
Ultra-violet if possible white ribbon/crêpe paper dance sticks *Polar bear*	Interactive dance. Practitioner imitates students' actions using dance sticks	Twinkly, sparkly, gentle arctic theme music
Finish	Holding/swaying/rocking together	Sing: (Tune: Row, Row the Boat). Rocking, singing time to say goodbye (rpt)
N.B. There should be enough props for child and practitioner to enable interactivity.		

Chapter 10

Finger dance

Finger dance is a programme using multisensory stimulus and playful games to develop a child's proprioceptive awareness and foster an ability to explore objects and mark-making materials. Undertaken at least weekly, it becomes a pleasant, familiar, relaxing routine. Some of the playful finger games include elements of anticipation to help arouse interest and a sense of playfulness. The key is to activate the proprioceptors (the little joints that send messages to your brain). This helps children to get to know where their hands and fingers are in relation to their body and this, in turn, may help a child explore objects more purposefully and enable them to 'make a mark on their world'.

We hold high expectations for our pre-intentional/pre-verbal children but, in truth, they are unlikely to progress to a stage where they will be able to write or, for some, even make an intentional mark on a piece of paper. Our focus, therefore, when considering pre-writing/mark-making is more likely to be concerned with developing self-awareness in relation to hands and fingers. Think hand–eye co-ordination, experimentation with various media, visual tracking, supported exploration and enabling a child to independently make a physical mark or change their immediate surroundings in some small way.

For more able children with learning difficulties it is important to remember that there are a number of prerequisite skills that a child has to acquire before they can write legibly and, importantly, an appropriate level of cognition and communication ability is paramount. Spatial awareness, an ability to track from left to right, visual perception (ability to interpret information visually) and appropriate posture are all prerequisite skills. Moreover, to write legibly children need to have an appreciation and awareness that words are made up of different sounds. They need to be able to hear and distinguish these different sounds in words. Once they have this understanding, learners need to be able to match these sounds to letter shapes and then go on to use this knowledge when they are reading and writing.

For practitioners working towards developing a child's interest in objects, the developmental checklist below may be helpful.

Developmental checklist – a child might:

- pay attention to own hands;
- play with finger moves showing some intentionality;
- show fleeting awareness of stimuli/object;
- glance towards or touch an object;
- briefly hold an object;
- hold and mouth an object;
- hold, mouth, glance at and inspect an object;

- hit, tap or throw an object;
- reach and grasp when an item is in view;
- observe properties of an object while exploring;
- show a growing interest in objects;
- track moving objects side to side and up and down;
- transfer object from hand to hand;
- engage in more complex exploration, e.g. shake, tap;
- search for an object dropped or hidden out of sight (object permanence);
- release an object to give;
- share an object with an adult (shared attention/joint attention);
- press, squeeze objects to test properties of object;
- discover function of object and practise skill, e.g. shake a shaker, bang a drum;
- consolidate and extend exploration with a variety of objects;
- name an object;
- practise in, on and under using objects (relational play/prepositions);
- begin to understand directionality: back, front, side etc.

Wiggling Fingers 'Song of Reference'

Figure 10.1 Wiggling Fingers

Programme/session plan

STEP 1

Basic weekly routine – proprioceptive workout	
Ideally, practitioner works one-to-one with a child	
Activity	**Resources/songs**
Song of reference Staff wiggle fingers towards and perhaps on children's hands.	Sing: Wiggling fingers ready to dance. Wiggling fingers twiddle and prance. Wiggling fingers before we can write. Wiggling fingers left and right.
Awaken Using gentle pressure on specific body parts to draw attention to these areas.	Accompany with light, pressured touch (cupped hand) using these words: 'From your shoulder, to your elbow to your wrist, to your hand, to your fingers' then repeat wiggling song
Finger massage Press, massage and pull each finger gently to stimulate proprioceptors.	Tune: 'Tommy Thumb' Feel your thumb, feel your thumb, tug and hug. (rpt) Continue using 'Feel your pointer – tall – ring and small' etc.
Body awareness/anticipation	Tune: 'Walking Round the Garden' All around your hand, skin and bone, forearm, upper arm and > > > under we go!

Programme/session plan

STEP 2

Additional activities: choose those that meet your requirements	
Activity	**Resources/songs**
Exploration/concept of objects Child-led play and exploration. Hand-under-hand, used thoughtfully, may help. Encourage squeeze action if possible. Prompt initially, if necessary, then withdraw.	A range of objects with different textures. I use a variety of balls but any sensory objects will do – perhaps those linked to a topic theme in schools/ Toys that squeak.
Hand rhymes To encourage tolerance of touch, sense of sequence, anticipation, imitation.	Use any other favourite or topic-linked rhymes and games incorporating hands/fingers.
Two hands It may help here to physically prompt, initially using a sensitive, hand-over-hand or simply prompting by supporting the elbow.	Use Clapping games, e.g. 'Clap your hand together 1, 2, 3 Clap your hands together you and me.' Small cymbals or other objects that can be played with or banged together.
Relaxation Cup the student's hand in your hands and squeeze, then release.	Saying: 'Squeeze > > > squeeze > > > > squeeze' in an exaggerated way and... Sigh out . . . 'Release'
Mark-making Enable the student to explore freely.	Use paint, flour, sand etc. – any sensory material.
Wave To encourage hand movement or gesture to signal goodbye.	Practitioners use wiggling fingers song to say goodbye: 'Wiggling fingers wave goodbye', etc

Extension ideas/activities

- Massage using cream.
- Story massage.
- Pointing games – try using a reception desk 'call bell'.
- Puppets or gloves to play and interact.
- Tickling feather games.
- Reach and grasp game-songs incorporating the use of a set of matching symbols or photographs to use within a picture trading system, e.g. PECS (Bondy and Frost, 1994).
- Mark-making or/and leaving a mark (e.g. manipulate a piece of material to create a visual change or hold and squeeze putty, clay, playdough).
- Isolate fingers to enable grasp. Try playing 'up and down the hill' game. Use your finger, start at the base of thumb and trace line of each finger saying 'up the hill, down the hill'.
- Action songs and movement rhymes that incorporate arm and upper-body movement.
- Some teachers use step one of the programme at the beginning of an art session.

Chapter 11

Story and drama

Telling tales – playing with words

Many stories have survived centuries: there are epics, myths, fairy stories, legends and fables; stories from around the world, new and old stories and literary tales – the list from which to choose seems endless.

Stories provide a wonderful tool for supporting literacy and topic work in schools and I particularly like the notion that closeness and nurture can be achieved using books and stories as a focus. Books are for *all* children: I recall, many years ago, a teacher who gathered children with SLD together in the quiet 'book corner' every morning to enjoy books. Most children were unable to read but were offered access to books and encouraged to explore them within the range of their ability and interest. Books were viewed, flicked, scratched or turned page-by-page. Some children were able to follow a storyline and one or two were emergent readers. Practitioners told stories and some children leant towards the practitioner during storytelling and in so doing were able to feel the vibration of the narrator's voice. An energy and warmth permeated this space and it made me realise that all children can access literature.

Stories create an atmosphere, images, curiosity and a sense of awe and wonder. They open up a world of wonderment full of the richness and diversity of words. Internal and external scenes recreate past, present and future landscapes as stories unfold – wonderful!

Story styles

Story styles used in special education with children with PMLD/SLD largely, but not exclusively, of course, fall into two categories: interactive and sensory, and these elements are usually combined.

Interactive stories

Interactive stories can be engaging and fun; in schools they are often used to introduce literature to children and to encourage the development of interaction and communication skills.

Teaching and learning

Eye contact can be encouraged in a natural and spontaneous way by using props and materials to draw attention to your face.

Anticipation games are included within the framework of the story: elements of horror, surprise and fun offer appropriate opportunities to create a song or chant using burst–pause strategies. This creates benefits in terms of learning about facial expressions and emotions and facilitates the development of signed/gestured and vocal responses.

Playfulness, fun and enjoyment enhance the story space serving to raise arousal levels and encourage a 'feel-good' factor within the group. This, in turn, helps to gain and maintain children's attention. Don't forget whispers, silence and gentleness as these are all part of the playfulness toolkit.

Vocalisations and movements generated by children can be incorporated into the story. By adding intention to vocalisations we acknowledge their input and teach children the message-carrying possibilities of their voice.

Gestures are acknowledged and responded to during the telling process. When a child reaches out, leans forward, nods or waves, for example, these moves are seen as signals with communicative intent. Wherever possible, these elements are brought into the story.

Sensory stories

Stories offer opportunities to deliver a sensory feast. Sensory elements can be woven into the story to awaken the senses: use touchy-feely games, visual props, auditory equipment, 'things' that smell and, when appropriate, perhaps something to taste.

The senses help children access information about the story, themselves and their world. Avoid a sensory onslaught, however, which may be frightening or threatening for some children. In truth, there is a need to be sensitive to individual children's responses at all times to keep them safe.

It is best to avoid overwhelming the story with too many props or objects; these should enhance the story scene rather than dominate.

Tactile elements can be threatening – children may dislike being touched; they may be tactile defensive, shy, anxious or simply unsure. Observe–think–assess and proceed carefully.

For children with PMLD, touch-speech cues, defined as 'a simultaneous touch-speech production in which the communication partner pairs a target word for comprehension with a specific touch signal on the individual's body or limb/s' (Goold and Hummell, 1993: 10) can be very helpful. In story terms touch-speech cues inform a child about what's coming next when visual/auditory senses are unrefined.

If and when appropriate, an element of rough-and-tumble may be relevant to a storyline (a rough and calm sea, for example) but again, when elements of touch are involved, sensitivity to a child's signals, likes and dislikes are essential.

Sense of **smell** varies from one person to another; thus, again, observation of children's responses is paramount. Bad smells like old blue cheese (smelly feet) or boiled eggs are just as useful as beautiful spices and likeable essences/perfumes.

Taste is closely linked with the development of smell. It is possible to increase a child's experience of the story through taste and texture but, again, care and sensitivity is required.

Visual stimulus and colours, in particular, can trigger a range of emotions from exhilaration to calmness. Material and all manner of colourful, black, white and metallic props help to gain and maintain a child's attention and reinforce the storyline. For some, the visual element will be important and some children may take a while to visually orientate their eyes. Consider lingering a while with certain materials to ensure appropriate access.

Auditory: vocal expressive sounds and music offer a means of developing interest and developing a greater understanding of the story. Play with dynamics to see what works well.

Simple sound output devices, e.g. Big Macs, can be useful for cause-and-effect experiences related to the auditory elements of the story – hand over hand is rarely helpful! Some sounds may offend, particularly with children with ASD, so again, great care is needed. Remember also the power of the sound of silence!

How to tell a story

To tell stories well is an art, but in truth, anyone can tell stories and I think, as practitioners, it is important to remember that storytelling becomes easier the more you tell. Take a risk and your confidence will grow. I view stories as a kind of soul food – here's my recipe:

- Gather ingredients (the story, props, material and music).
- Mix, stir and mould to meet your needs.
- Add your amazing personality and zest (your secret ingredient).
- '*Voila*', you have created a story feast.

Figure 11.1 Storyland

The basics

- Find a story (libraries, internet, children's books, and beg, 'steal' and borrow stories from other practitioners). Choose stories that *you* really like.
- Consider the audience, their ability and learning needs and adjust planning accordingly.
- Consider the environment for 'telling'. Some stories benefit from a changed venue: soft play area, light and sound, room or outside area. Move to a different place in the classroom or tell a story on the move.
- Consider the use of music, songs, poetry, chants, rhymes and anticipation games as part of the storytelling process.
- Make/acquire props and consider any other suitable sensory items or materials that could enhance elements of the story. Become a junk junkie – collect together all kinds of materials, hats, gloves, puppets and so on. Choose props to encourage active participation from children.
- Preparation/consider storage of props and sensory materials – keep in a bag or box to draw out when needed during the telling.
- Tell the story out loud to yourself and begin to refine your technique.

Golden rules

- Become a story hoarder – beg, 'steal' and borrow stories to create your own wonderful, story resource file.
- Plan to tempt, tease, surprise, invite, intrigue and offer choices.
- Learn by telling – refine and tell again – stories have a basic storyline. Your version of the story will be unique but don't lose the 'thread' and focal theme during the telling.
- Each storyteller brings their own personality and unique style to enhance the story space – hoorah!
- Work intuitively – use your senses to 'suss out' the audience.
- Try things out and take risks but learn from your mistakes.
- The children will tell you what they like if you observe their behaviour and note negative and positive signals.
- When children enjoy a particular element, put more emphasis on this element during the next telling. Equally, if some elements appear to drag or if children show disinterest, minimise this element on the next telling.
- Adjust practices to ensure children are active and not passive during the process.
- Be animated, interesting and different – use dynamic interludes to drive the pulse of the story and collaborate with the audience.
- Enjoy – if you show your 'real' enjoyment, children will pick up on this vibe and enjoy the story too.
- Encourage others to have a go.
- When you are ready to begin 'telling', make sure children are ready too, and as attentive as possible. It's a good idea to use a gathering 'song of reference' (something like: 'Story time, story time, come and join me now – shh, listen') to help focus attention.

Extension ideas/activities

- Consider all practitioners having a set of story props to aid the flow and maximise interaction.
- Props can be used to retell the story to an individual.
- Follow-up work might include art experiences.
- Use dance work (interactive musical movement) to capture and express central story themes.
- Make an audio copy of the story for individual listening.
- Make a big book, tactile story books or board games using story themes.
- Worksheets may be appropriate for some.
- Use songs and activities in other settings.

Drama

Preparation for drama, in PMLD/SLD settings, follows similar lines to storytelling but children are usually encouraged to be more physically active and directly involved in the dramatisation of a story. They have roles, dress up, maybe, and portray characteristics of story characters. In dramatic production there has to be a director and thus child-centeredness tends to slip into second place. Drama can work well when practitioners dress up and act out roles. This can be fun and engaging for the 'audience' and help to embed in children a real sense of the storyline.

Basics

- Begin the drama together: sitting on a bench, a circle of chairs, bean bags or a designated mat.
- Use cues – visual, verbal, gestural/signing – to inform moves. Keep language simple (key words). State your expectation to ensure practitioners know their roles and responsibilities in the management and facilitation of the ongoing drama and encourage them to facilitate each child's active (and independent whenever possible) participation.
- Make sure everyone is ready to start – attention is key.
- Strategies to keep and hold attention such as using a count of 5 4 3 2 1 or hands-in-the-air signal can be helpful throughout the drama session for more able children.
- Have a plan but let the story develop over several weeks as children's strengths and difficulties are embraced and special skills included and fostered.
- Use genuine praise often – it's not easy being an actor!

Sensory/Interactive Story: Rhama and Sita

Overview: This Hindu story is adapted for use with children with PMLD/SLD and is most suitable for use during the Hindu Festival of Light – Divali.	
Activities	**Resources**
Sari waft to gentle Indian audio music	Indian CD, saris
Sing: 'Time for Divali, Oh Yes' (Gilbert, 2009: 59)	Indian puppets to dance around
Spoken narrative: 'In a cottage in the forest Rhama and Sita'. Branches wafted around children	Branches dipped in suitable essential oil
Sing: 'Where's the Demon King'. Spooky interaction	Blackout: masks and torches
Spoken narrative: 'STOP, STOP, the Demon King has got Sita'. Wheelchair dance or play a 'got you' game	Appropriate audio music
Spoken narrative: 'Call the Monkey King and all the monkeys into battle'. Body drama: tap gently on body parts to rhythm	Bollywood music or similar.
Spoken narrative: 'Rhama and Sita are safe – they sail away together on the back of a beautiful white swan'. White feather blown, or tickling games with feathers	Gentle audio music
Quiet reflective time: Black out – opportunity for gentle movement work	Divali music Battery-operated tea-lights
Celebration/dancing	Audio-CD 'Bollywood' tinsel and sensory props

Chapter 12

Artwork

I like Martinovich's (2006: 259) suggestion that art experiences offer children opportunities to express themselves in direct, spontaneous ways. In this chapter the word 'themselves' is stressed because all too often SLD/PMLD artwork is co-produced by helpers who strive to make art acceptable and presentable by adding something to it. Such additions are probably associated with our own desire for harmony and balance but when children's work is 'doctored', art becomes an exercise concerned with product and not process. Helping children too much during the process is likely to result in a diminished experience for budding artists. I hold no high ground here because I am guilty of succumbing to the urge to add this or that to spruce up artwork. I am, however, trying to be more mindful to ensure art generates from the child alone during the process.

Another popular practice concerns practitioners cutting out children's artwork to create a desired shape. This can produce nice effects but I think we need to be careful not to devalue the child's art effort. When artwork looks like it has been produced by practitioners, it probably has!

In truth 'producing' art can be problematic, and for some children with PMLD almost physically impossible. So... this is the challenge to practitioners: how to facilitate independent, active participation that enables each child to produce something resonating with their own experience. The quality of facilitation and interaction during the art-making process is thus paramount: quietening our inner voice; going with the child's flow; willing them on without using words; adoring their art work even and reinforcing their efforts wholeheartedly. All this helps practitioners to remain in the moment – the moment of creation!

Art is a process for practitioner as well as the child. The practitioner thinks about the material before an art session and applies creative thoughtfulness to the task in hand: they are going through their own creative process. For example, when an elephant provides the motivation to produce art, the subject matter is kept in mind during planning and when choosing materials. The practitioner thinks colour, texture, shape, noise, size and movement and finds imaginative resources to encourage active, artistic expression.

Art for children with SLD/PMLD is essentially about encounter; giving experiences that will enable them to visualise and create an image. Body language, vocalisations and actions all form part of the interactional journey.

> Creating art is about interacting with the materials at hand and valuing the results as they are.

Practitioner voice

A recent conversation with an experienced artist was helpful. She talked about art being a process of the heart suggesting that there needs to be empathy between the 'artist practitioner' and the child artist. Art, she suggested, is about individual interpretation, reaction and response; it involves a direct correlation between what a child does physically and the resulting artwork. The interaction within the process is viewed as most important.

The process of art, then, is interactive and creative; it's about bringing materials together into a form or pattern and, importantly, for 'our' children, it's about making their mark. In our specialised world, there will inevitably be a collaborative or participatory factor in the process of producing art but intervention is best when it concerns sensitive acts of facilitation – playful whenever possible – so that, ultimately, the art is shaped by the child. 'What happens depends on the learner's own interests; the emphasis is on the exploring, the doing, the discovery' (Nind and Hewett, 2005: 13).

The notion of calling something 'art' is fascinating. I tend to cling to the old adage 'Beauty is in the eye of the beholder'. In schools, where artwork is often produced to deck the halls and walls, the skill of what I call the window dresser/designer, most likely holds the key to beauty! Head teacher and art therapist David Reid has taught me a great deal about celebrating children's artwork. His insight and creativity have helped me to understand that the co-active art process begins once the child has completed their 'masterpiece'. To display children's artwork in its raw state is, of course, appropriate and valuable but sometimes art can be made more aesthetically pleasing by framing. Most painters, after all, frame their art. The designer (practitioner) has the task of creating a display or framing a piece of art work to 'show off' a child's achievements and I have called this constructive framing.

Constructive framing

Constructive framing involves a certain amount of ingenuity, imagination and flair. It involves taking children's original artwork and framing it, individually or collectively.

Choice of framing is important and it benefits a practitioner to think outside the box. Fabricate, formulate, produce, put together – the aim is to make the artwork aesthetically pleasing without losing any of the child's mark-making and originality. Think big, small, tall, three-dimensional/two-dimensional and take note of and use ideas from other artists, galleries and shop-window displays.

Chapter 13

Reflective circle

Figure 13.1 Reflective circle

Spirituality

Reflective circle offers a quality intimate space where a variety of faiths can be explored sensitively through creative and sensory experiences. Attention to the spiritual/religious orientation of individual group members is, of course, essential. There is a wealth of tradition to draw upon and it is helpful to encourage children and staff to be respectful towards all faith and non-faith backgrounds.

Insight and wisdom from faith and non-faith traditions help to create a canvas of colour and this provides a backdrop for concepts such as honour, dignity, love and hope. This is a reflective group not collective worship – a journey of discovery inwards involving the senses, spirit, thoughts and ideas. Children are given the opportunity to become involved and active in the process of stillness and reflection; they are taught about faith traditions through the senses, religious artefacts, ritual, symbolism, celebration and silence.

Setting

Reflective circle provides an opportunity for children with PMLD/SLD to explore spirituality within a daily or weekly class session. There is a set time (around 20 minutes) and basic circle structure, which offers a sense of inclusion and aids joint focus and shared attention.

Circle

A circle is a powerful symbol used by people for hundreds of years. A poignant symbol of eternity, the circle holds no sense of hierarchy; standing or sitting we are united as one group. Being one, but part of a whole, we can engage on many levels and acknowledge others beside and opposite. While sitting in a circle, our eyes and minds are drawn, quite naturally, to the centre. Whether full or empty the inner circle provides a focal point and opportunities for joint attention.

Sensory

A small, visually accessible table can provide the central feature for a reflective circle. This is 'dressed' to suit weekly or daily themes. For example, drape with a colourful sari, prayer mat, table cloth or particular piece of material that reflects and links nicely to a particular theme. Place relevant items and sensory stimuli on the table that link with the theme as this will serve to bathe and awaken the senses. Perhaps something to touch, smell, taste and listen to. A lit candle in the centre of the table can aid awareness and serves to draw children's eyes towards the centre. Subdued or coloured spotlighting can also enhance the space.

Language in context

Use short simple phrases and limit words. Key words and phrases such as 'think, quiet, calm, listen, be still, listen with your heart' can help to establish a routine and reinforce what is happening. Ensure a 'total communication approach' (signing, symbols, touch cues and simple spoken language) to ensure inclusion and maximise learning opportunities. This time is separate and distinct from the rest of the school day. The session concerns contemplation, discovery, exploring and retrieving thoughts in an attempt to foster within children a sense of self, community and global awareness.

Silence

Stillness and silence create space in a busy world. Where there is silence, there is an opportunity for body and mind to become calm and this creates an opening for peaceful reflection. An atmosphere that includes silence helps children travel inwards, to listen to their inner voice and to search their hearts and minds for meaning and identity.

Celebration

While silence is a powerful reflective tool, sounds and visual stimuli create an atmosphere and enhance moods. Different themes create different moods and for our children it is appropriate to embrace a particular theme in a multifaceted way. Shades of dark and light, sound and silence, stillness and movement, colour and contrast, all enhance the reflective space. And yes, playfulness has a role to play too!

Creative arts

Embedded within the process, as and when appropriate, are elements of music, art, drama, poetry, movement, dance, story, signs and symbols, meditation, prayer, visualisation, mantra, incense, blessings and procession.

Themes

A number of symbolic themes permeate most world faiths: light, fire and water, for example, and many faith traditions offer thanksgiving for agriculture and harvest. These elements can be sensitively infused into the process of reflective circle to reflect a particular religious festival. A seasonal focus and themes from the natural world also work well.

Chapter 14

Final thoughts

My final thoughts are for you – practitioners working, caring or living with children with PMLD/SLD/ASD.

The day-to-day care of these very precious individuals is potentially difficult: demanding, monotonous, physically challenging and, at times, frustrating. Sessions, even creative ones, often fail to go as planned because of interruptions, medical or personal care issues, staff shortages, challenging behaviour and so on. Teamwork is often the key to survival – a place where everyone feels valued, where practitioner's skills are recognised and used to aid teaching and learning, and where open dialogue serves to create a strong, supportive, caring, knowledgeable team. Everyone has a role to play and everyone has a responsibility to make the team work well. Good leadership is central. When a leader is willing to work alongside colleagues, lead by example, communicate, share knowledge and show that they genuinely value team members, everyone benefits. A shared vision that promotes active listening, quality interaction, a total communication approach and playful endeavour enables everyone's voice to be heard including, and especially, the children.

Of course, time spent with these special children can be rewarding, joyous, satisfying and fun; they have an innocence that seems to connect to the very core of our being and their ability to make other people feel special is stunning.

Many practitioners are passionate about their work and I applaud their dedication and ability to cope with the sometimes unrealistic demands placed on them by those who insist children with PMLD/SLD/ASD should be routinely judged by monitoring and assessment systems that fail to recognise the fundamental and often disjointed nature of their individual abilities. A valued colleague of mine, Laura Blake, has some helpful thoughts regarding the assessment of children with PMLD. She reminded me that 'we are constantly assessing what we deliver', and that 'each interaction requires reflection and response' – what she likes to think of as 'reflective action'. It is this reflective action that guides the process, moves a child forward and differentiates the playful, interactive processes from entertainment. Assessment, then, is important but as Laura explained 'It's just that the tools we use are sometimes problematic'.

I hope this book gives you permission to be playful. I want to put fire in your belly, to stir you up, so that you question everything about your practice. I want this book to encourage you to adopt an experimental frame of mind so that the space you create for children is full of playfulness, fun, interest, creativity, respect and an abundance of quality interaction.

Figure 14.1 Follow me

Guide to other resources

Intensive interaction

Firth, G. and Barber, M. (2010) *How to Use 'Intensive Interaction' with a Person with a Social or Communicative Impairment*, London: Jessica Kingsley.

Firth, G., Berry, R. and Irvine, C. (2010) *Understanding Intensive Interaction*, London: Jessica Kingsley.

Hewett, D. (ed.) (forthcoming) *Intensive Interaction: Theoretical Perspectives*, London: Sage.

Hewett, D., Barber, M., Firth, G. and Irvine, C. (forthcoming) *The Intensive Interaction Handbook*, London: Sage.

Hewett, D. and Nind, M. (eds) (1998) *Interaction in Action: Reflections on the Use of Intensive Interaction*, London: David Fulton. (See, in particular, chapter by Val Stothard.)

Kellett, M. and Nind, M. (2003) *Implementing Intensive Interaction in Schools: Guidance for Practitioners, Managers and Coordinators*, London: David Fulton.

Nind, M. and Hewett, D. (1994) *Access to Communication: Developing the Basics of Communication with People with Severe Learning Difficulties through Intensive Interaction*, London: David Fulton.

Nind, M. and Hewett, D. (2001) *A Practical Guide to Intensive Interaction*, Kidderminster: British Institute of Learning Disabilities.

Nind, M. and Hewett, D. (2005) *Access to Communication: Developing the Basics of Communication with People with Severe Learning Difficulties through Intensive Interaction*, 2nd edn. London: David Fulton.

Rhodes, J. and Hewett, D. (2010) 'The human touch: physical contact and making a social world available for the most profoundly disabled', *PMLD Link*, 22 (2), 11–14.

The British Institute of Learning Disabilities (BILD) website: www.bild.org.uk/pdfs/05faqs/ii.pdf

The official 'Intensive Interaction' website: www.IntensiveInteraction.co.uk

The Intensive Interaction Regional Support Group: http://www.intensiveinteraction.co.uk/regional-networks/

The Leeds Partnerships NHS Trust's Intensive Interaction webpage where you can download the most recent issue of the UK Intensive Interaction Newsletter (http://www.leedspft.nhs.uk/our_services/ld/intensiveinteraction).

Us in a Bus www.usinabus.org

Play/playfulness

Christie, P., Newson, E., Prevezer, W. and Chandler, S. (2009) *First Steps in Intervention with Your Child with Autism: Frameworks for Communication*. London: Jessica Kingsley.

Early Years: an international journal of research and development (http://www.tandf.co.uk/journals/ceye).

Parker-Rees, R. (1999) 'Protecting playfulness', in L. Abbott and H. Moylett (eds) *Early Education Transformed*, London: Falmer, pp. 61–72.

Parker-Rees, R. (2000) 'Time to relax a little: making time for the interplay of minds in education', *Education 3–13, 28* (1): 29–35.

Parker-Rees, R. (2007) 'Liking to be liked: imitation, familiarity and pedagogy in the first years of life', *Early Years*, 27 (1): 3–17.

Parker-Rees, R. (2010) 'Hunting and gathering: how play helps us to let in, as well as to get in, information about our environment', in J. Moyles (ed.) *The Excellence of Play*, 3rd edn. OU/McGraw-Hill.

Parker-Rees, R. (2011) *Meeting the Child in Steiner Kindergartens*, London: Taylor Francis Ltd.

Play Therapy United Kingdom (PTUK) www.playtherapy.org.uk

Seach, D. (2011) (in press) *Interactive Play and Creative Activities for Children with Autism and Asperger's Syndrome*, London: Taylor and Francis.

The International Journal of Play (http://www.tandf.co.uk/journals/RIJP).

US Play Association TASP (The Association for the Study of Play) (http://www.tasplay.org/about.html).

Music

Bean, J. and Oldfield, A. (2001) *Pied Piper: Musical Activities to Develop Basic Skills*, London: Jessica Kingsley.

Insight magazine, RNIB.

Lloyd, P. (2008) *Songs for Group Work in Settings that Include Students with Learning Difficulties and Autism*, London: Jessica Kingsley.

Logan, N. (2004) 'Rock-a-bye-Blues: music as a tool for parents', *PMLD Link*, 16 (3), issue 49

Ockelford, A. (1996) *All Join in!*, London: RNIB.

Ockelford, A. (2008) *Music for Children and Young People with Complex Needs*, Oxford: Oxford University Press.

Orr, R. (2003) *My Right to Play: A Child with Complex Needs*, Maidenhead: Open University Press.

Paterson, A. and Zimmermann, S. (eds) (2006) *No Need For Words: Special Needs in Music Education*, Matlock: NAME.

Prevezer, W. (2002) *Entering into Interaction*, available from the Elizabeth Newson Centre, 272 Longdale Lane, Ravenshead, Nottingham NG15 9AH. Tel: 01623 490879.

Rock-a-Bye Blues (CD) (www.juliewyliemusic.com).

Shephard, C. and Stormont, B. (2005) *Jabulani!*, Stroud: Hawthorn Press.

Welch, G., Ockelford, A. and Zimmermann, S.A. (2001) *PROMISE: Provision of Music in Special Education*, London: RNIB and Institute of Education.

www.ambertrust.org – a charity supporting blind and partially sighted children of any ability in their music-making.

www.skooqmusic.com – an exciting new musical instrument.

www.soundabout.org.uk – an organisation aiming at 'using music to unlock the potential of young people with severe disabilities'.

www.soundsofintent.org – Sounds of Intent – promoting children's engagement with music.

Dance and drama

Tortora, S. (2006) *The Dancing Dialogue: Using the Communicative Power of Movement with Young Children*, Baltimore, MD: Paul H. Brookes Publishing Company.
www.jabadeo.org – JABADEO – National Centre for Movement, Learning and Health.
www.oilycart.org.uk – Oily Cart Theatre Company.

Bibliography

Ayres, A. J. (1979) *Sensory Integration and the Child*, Los Angeles, CA: Western Psychological Services.

Berger, S. D. (2002) *Music Therapy, Sensory Integration and the Autistic Child*, London: Jessica Kingsley.

Bondy, A. S. and Frost, L. A. (1994) 'The picture exchange communication system', *Focus on Autism and Other Developmental Disabilities*, 9 (3), 1–19.

Bruner, J. (1982) 'The organisation of action and the nature of adult–infant transaction', in M. Von Cranach and R. Harre (eds) *The Analysis of Action*. New York: Cambridge University Press, pp. 313–27.

Bruner, J. S. (1990) *Acts of Meaning*, Cambridge, MA: Harvard University Press.

Bruner, J. S. (2006) *In Search of Pedagogy, Volume 11*, Abingdon: Routledge.

Burningham, J. (1991) *Oi! Get Off Our Train*, Salisbury: Red Fox.

Cases, A. K. (2003) [online] 'Childhood playfulness as a predictor of adult playfulness and creativity: a longitudinal study', Masters thesis submitted to the Faculty of the Virginias Polytechnic Institute and State University in partial fulfilment of the requirements for the degree of Masters in Science in Child Development. Available from Google Scholar (accessed on 17/4/06).

The Children's Society 'Good Childhood Inquiry' summary (www.goodchildhood.org.uk). Accessed 23/6/07.

Contact Improvisation UK (contactimprovisation.co.uk). Accessed online 2/1/11.

Corke, M. (2002) *Approaches to Communication through Music*, London: David Fulton Publishers.

Corke, M. (2007) 'Exploring practitioner playfulness within a primary school', unpublished dissertation, University of Chichester.

Crichton, S. and Greenland, P. (1994) *First Moves Movement Work with Very Young Children: A Handbook for Play Workers and Teachers*. a JABADAO publication (currently out of print). To access information online: jabadeo.org

Csikszentmihalyi, M. (1975) *Beyond Boredom and Anxiety*, San Francisco, CA: Jossey-Bass.

Csikszentmihalyi, M. (1996) *Creativity: Flow and the Psychology of Discovery and Invention*, New York: Harper Collins.

DCSF (2004) Children's Act. Department for Children, Schools and Families (dcsf.gove.uk/childrenactreport).

Dewey, J. (1933) *How We Think*, New York: Houghton Mifflin.

DFE (2008) *The Early Years Foundation Stage: Setting the Standards for Learning, Development and Care for Children from Birth to Five* (http://nationalstrategies.standards.dcsf.gove.uk?node/157774). Accessed 18/3/2011.

DFE (2009) EYFS *Learning, Playing and Interacting: Good Practice in the Early Years Foundation Stage* (nationalstrategies.standards.dcsf.gov.uk/node/242798). Accessed on 18/3/2011.

Finnegan, R. (2002) *Communicating: The Multiple Modes of Human Interconnectedness*, London: Routledge.

Fogel, A. (1993) *Developing through Relationships*, Chicago, IL: The University of Chicago Press.

Frith, U. (2003) *Autism: Explaining the Enigma*, 2nd edn. Oxford: Blackwell Publishing.

Gerdhardt, S. (2003) *Why Love Matters: How Affection Shapes a Baby's Brain*. London: Taylor & Francis.

Gerdhardt, S. (2010) *Selfish Society*. London: Simon and Schuster.

Gilbert, J. (2009) *Festivals*. Oxford: Oxford University Press.

Glynn, M. A. and Webster, J. (1992) 'The adult playfulness scale: an initial assessment', *Psychological Reports*, 71: 83–103.

Goold, L. and Hummell, J. (1993) *Supporting the Receptive Communication of Individuals with Significant Multiple Disabilities: Selective Use of Touch to Enhance Comprehension*, North Rocks 2151, Australia: North Rocks Press.

Hewett, D. (2006) 'The most important and complicated learning: that's what play is for!' (http://talkingpoint.org.uk/info). Accessed on 8/2/06)

Hewett, D. (2011) 'Issues around what is called "age-appropriateness",' in *The Intensive Interaction Newsletter*, Leeds Partnership Foundation Trust, 34, winter, p. 3.

Hewett, D. Intensive Interaction website (intensiveinteraction.co.uk). Accessed 8/5/11.

Hobson, P. (2002) *The Cradle of Thought*, London: Pan Macmillan Ltd.

Huss, A. J. (1977) 'Touch with care or caring touch', *American Journal of Occupational Therapy*, 31, 295–309.

Jabadao – Developmental Movement Play Theory (www.jabdao.org.dmptheory). Accessed 18/11/08.

Kellet, M. and Nind, M. (2003) *Implementing Intensive Interaction in Schools*. London: David Fulton Publishers.

Laban, R. (1948) *Modern Educational Dance*. London: MacDonald and Evans.

Lieberman, J. N. (1977) *Playfulness: Its Relationship to Imagination and Creativity*, London: Academic Press.

Martinovich, J. (2006) *Creative Expressive Activities and Asperger's Syndrome*. London: Jessica Kingsley.

Maslow, A. H. (1987) *Motivation and Personality*, 3rd edn. New York: Harper Collins.

Maxwell, S., Reed, G., Saker, J. and Story, V. (2005) 'The two faces of playfulness: a new tool to select potentially successful sales reps', *Journal of Personal Selling and Sales Management*, 25 (3): 215–29 (available also from Google Scholar).

Menuhin, Y. (1979) *The Music of Man*. University of Michigan: Methuen Publishing Ltd.

McLinden, M. and McCall, S. (2002) *Learning through Touch: Supporting Children with Visual Impairment and Additional Difficulties*. London: David Fulton Publishers.

Meltz and Lutz (1990), cited in J. R. Moyles (1994) *The Excellence of Play*, Buckingham: Open University Press.

Mount, M. K. (2005) *Exploring the Role of Self-disclosure and Playfulness in Adult Attachment Relationships* (drum.lib.umd.edu/bitstream/1903/2928/1/umi-2719.pdf). Accessed 18/3/2011.

Morreall (1987), cited in *Internet Encyclopaedia of Philosophy*, 'Humour' (www.iep.utm.edu/h/humour.htm). Accessed on 4/9/2006.

Naess, J. (1982) 'Developmental approaches to interactive process in dance/movement therapy', *American Journal of Dance Therapy*, 5: 43–55.

National Children's Bureau (2006) 'Play theories and the value of play' (www.ncb.org.uk). Accessed 12/6/2006.

Nind, M. and Hewett, D. (1994) *Access to Communication*. London: David Fulton Publishers.

Nind, M. and Hewett, D. (2005) *Access to Communication*, 2nd edn., London: David Fulton Publishers.

Ockleford, A. (2008) *Music for Children and Young People with Complex Needs*, Oxford: Oxford University Press.

Panksepp, J. (1998) *Affective Neuroscience: The Foundations of Human and Animal Emotions*, Oxford: Oxford University Press.

Parks, S. (1994) 'Hawaii Early Learning Profile'. Palo Alto, CA: VORT Corporation.

Parker-Rees, R. (1999) 'Protecting playfulness', in L. Abbott and H. Moylett (eds) *Early Education Transformed*. London: Routledge Falmer.

Parker-Rees, R. (2000) 'Supporting playful learning communities in staffrooms and classrooms', paper presented at BERA 2000, Cardiff. Available from Rolle School of Education, University of Plymouth.

Parker-Rees, R. (2004) 'Moving, playing and learning: children's active exploration of their world', in Willan, J., Parker-Rees, R. and Savage, J. *Early Childhood Studies*. Exeter: Learning Matters.

Parker-Rees, R. (2007) 'Primary communication – what can adults learn from babies?', in J. Moyles (ed.) *Early Years: Challenges and Issues*. Open University/McGraw-Hill, pp. 24–36.

Pollard, A. (2005) *Reflective Teaching,* 2nd edn., London: Continuum.

Prevezer, W. (1991) 'Musical interaction', *Speech and Language Disorders Newsletter*, 37: 10–11.

Prevezer, W. (2000) 'Musical interaction and children with autism', in S. Powell (ed.) *Helping Children with Autism to Learn*, London: David Fulton Publishers.

Prevezer, W. (2002) *Entering into Interaction* (unpublished). Available from The Early Years Diagnostic Centre, Nottinghamshire.

QCA (2005) 'Creativity: find it, promote it! – promoting pupils' creative thinking and behaviour across the curriculum at key stages 1, 2 and 3 – practical materials for schools', London: Qualifications and Curriculum Authority.

Reddy, V. and Trevarthen, C. (2004) 'What we learn about babies from engaging with their emotions', *Zero to Three*, 24 (3), 9–15.

Routes for Learning (2006) Qualifications and Curriculum Group, Lifelong Learning and Skills, Wales. Crown Copyright. Copies of the Routes for Learning pack can be obtained from the Qualifications and Curriculum Group, Department for Education, Lifelong Learning and Skills, Wales.

Scarlet, G. W., Naudeau, S., Salonius-Pasternak, D. and Ponte, I. (2005) *Children's Play*, London: Sage Publications.

Schaffer, H. R. (1998) *Social Development*, Oxford: Blackwell Publishers.

Sharon, H. (1987) *Changing Children's Minds*, London: Souvenir Press.

Sherborne, V. (2001) *Developmental Movement for Children*, 2nd edn., Worth Publishing Ltd, England.

Smith, D. (1995) 'How play influences children's development at home and school', *Journal of Physical Education, Recreation and Dance*, 66 (8): 19.

Sonders, S. A. (2003) *Giggle Time: Establishing the Social Connection*, London: Jessica Kingsley.

Stern, D. N. (1977) *The First Relationship*. Cambridge, MA: Harvard University Press.

Stern, D. N. (1985) *The Interpersonal World of the Infant*. New York: Basic Books.

Stern, D. N., Beebe, B., Jaffe, J. and Bennett, S. L. (1977) 'The infants' stimulus world during social interaction: a study of caregiver behaviours with particular reference to repetition and timing', in H. R. Schaffer (eds) *Studies in Mother–Infant Interaction*, London: Academic Press.

Strickland, D. (1993) 'Seriously, laughter matters', *Today's OR Nurse*, Nov./Dec.

Trevarthen, C. (2002) 'Origins of musical identity: evidence from infancy for musical social awareness', in R. A. R. MacDonalds, D. J. Hargreaves and D. Miell (eds) *Musical Identities*, Oxford: Oxford University Press.

Vygotsky, L. S. (1978) *Mind in Society: The Development of Higher Psychological Processes*, Cambridge: MA: Harvard University Press.

Wimpory, D. C. and Nash, S. (1999) 'Musical interaction therapy: therapeutic play for children with autism', *Child Language Teaching and Therapy*, 15 (1): 17–28.

Wing, L. (1996) *The Autistic Spectrum*, London: Constable and Robinson.

Winnicott, D. W. (1971, 2005) *Playing and Reality*, London: Brunner Routledge.

Index